round loom KNITTING
in 10 easy lessons

30 Stylish Projects

Nicole F. Cox

STACKPOLE BOOKS

Lanham   Boulder   New York   London

Published by Stackpole Books
An imprint of Globe Pequot
Trade Division of The Rowman & Littlefield Publishing Group, Inc.
4501 Forbes Boulevard, Suite 200, Lanham, Maryland 20706
www.rowman.com

Distributed by National Book Network

Printed in the United States of America

First edition

Cover design by Caroline M. Stover
Photography by Nicole F. Cox

Library of Congress Cataloging-in-Publication Data

Names: Cox, Nicole F., author.
Title: Round loom knitting in 10 easy lessons : 30 stylish projects / Nicole
    F. Cox.
Other titles: Round loom knitting in ten easy lessons
Description: First edition. | Mechanicsburg, PA : Stackpole Books, 2016.
Identifiers: LCCN 2015047859 | ISBN 9780811716499 (pbk.) | ISBN 9780811764834
(electronic)
Subjects: LCSH: Knitting—Patterns. | Handlooms.
Classification: LCC TT825 .C7275 2016 | DDC 746.43/2041—dc23 LC record available
at http://lccn.loc.gov/2015047859

round loom KNITTING
in 10 easy lessons

For my daughters, Amber and Danielle, my husband, Ray,
and my "brothers," Warren and Charlie,
who are an endless source of love, joy, and support.

CONTENTS

vi

ACKNOWLEDGMENTS

A special thanks to:

- My editors, Pam Hoenig and Candi Derr, for their guidance and faith in me through-out this journey. Thank you for giving me the creative freedom I needed to complete this book.

- My husband and daughters for their help with lighting, photography, proofreading, styling, and their endless encouragement.

- My models, Amber Cox, Danielle Cox, Greg Pretti, McKenna Coffey, Lily Adair, Michael Lenhardt, and Manuel Montoya. Thank you for enduring snow, wind, and a blinding reflector in your eyes.

- CinDWood and Cottage Looms for supplying some of the looms used in this book; your looms are a joy to work with.

- The loom knitting community; without you, this book never would have happened.

INTRODUCTION

Welcome to the world of loom knitting! The round or circular loom is a versatile knitting tool, opening up the door to almost any knitting project. Looms come in many shapes (circular, rectangular, figure 8, flower) and sizes, with various names, including knitting board, knitting rake, and knitting loom. As a pattern designer, I find the circular or round looms to be the most versatile. You can knit in the round for circular items such as hats and socks, as well as do flat panel knitting for items like scarves. The list of garments and items that can be worked on the round loom is endless—sweaters, slippers, blankets, shawls, totes, toys, and so much more.

The round loom is easy to hold and easy to master, making it a wonderful choice for younger or first-time needlecrafters. Those without the dexterity or patience for needle knitting will find that it's easy to create even stitches on the round loom, allowing them to knit beautiful, well-made items.

The art of loom knitting is growing in popularity because it fits into today's busy lifestyle. It is much faster than traditional needle knitting; small projects, like a slouchy hat, can be completed in less than two hours. There is also a wide range of stitches that can be worked on the loom, so the knitter will not become bored. Loom knitting is the perfect creative outlet for even the most hectic schedule!

This book will take you through a series of ten lessons that build upon each other, taking you from absolute beginner to more advanced skills. At the end of each lesson, there are two patterns that make use of the skills you've just learned, as well as draw on the skills from earlier lessons. At the end of the book are ten bonus patterns that will allow you to further your creativity.

My step-by-step approach is designed to build confidence in the loom knitter. Full online video support for all the techniques used in this book is available on my YouTube Channel at https://www.youtube.com/channel/UCmxMjIq7uUsTIa2JxDtygxQ.

If you are already an experienced loom knitter, use the book as a convenient reference and enjoy the 30 stylish original designs it includes.

Thank you for joining me in this adventure. Soon you'll be proud to say, "I'm a loom knitter."

Happy loom knitting!

Nicole F. Cox

Getting Started in Round Loom Knitting

oom knitting is the art of creating woven fabric using pegs set into a frame instead of traditional knitting needles. It is helpful to think of the pegs as your knitting needles. Before you begin your lessons in round loom knitting, you need a round loom. As the name suggests, round looms are circular. Looms are manufactured in plastic and wood, with the pegs being made of wood, plastic, or metal. The plastic circular loom is widely found in local craft stores and is the most commonly used by beginners; it's also usually the most affordable.

Round looms come in many different diameters, with different numbers of pegs set into the frame (from 12 to more than 100), with different spacings between the pegs (see page 131 for my helpful charts, Guide to Popular Round Looms and Loom Comparison by Peg Spacing and Number of Pegs). Circular looms can be bought

Here is a small sample of the types of round looms currently available.

individually or in sets that include different sizes. One of the challenges of round loom knitting is that there is no standardization of sizes across manufacturers; one brand may sell a set of looms with diameters of 5.5"/14 cm, 7.5"/19 cm, 9.5"/24 cm, and 11.5"/29 cm, and a set from another brand will be 5"/12.5 cm, 7"/18 cm, 9"/23 cm, and 11"/28 cm.

Let's first examine the anatomy of a round loom and its use.

Loom Anatomy

These are the features that make up the loom:

1. **Holding peg:** Used to hold the working yarn at the beginning of your project.
2. **Peg:** Used to hold the yarn, allowing you to make various stitches.
3. **Peg spacing:** This is the distance between two pegs; measured from the center of a peg to the center of the next peg, this distance determines gauge. Unfortunately, round loom manufacturers don't usually indicate the gauge of their looms. You'll need to take this measurement yourself.
4. **Base:** This is the backbone of your loom. It holds the pegs firmly in place and acts as a handle for the knitter.
5. **Knob:** Keeps the yarn from slipping off the peg.
6. **Groove:** Facilitates easier lifting of the yarn.

Take time to research the type of loom you wish to knit with. All loomers have their favorite brands of looms, with each having its pros and cons. Go online and check the reviews for the looms you are considering. Things to take into account include: durability, whether the base requires maintenance (sanding or staining for a wooden base), diameter, gauge, type of pegs (wood, plastic, metal), type of groove on the peg, size of the knobs, and the overall weight of the loom.

When shopping for a loom, it's important to know the weight of the yarn you are likely to be using with it, as you will need to buy a loom with a gauge appropriate to that yarn. If you are interested in knitting bulky knits, then a set of large-gauge looms would be appropriate, but if you love delicate, lacy knits, you may want to consider small- to fine-gauge looms. The table on page 4 will help you determine what gauge loom is best suited to different weights of yarn. Many companies sell sets of round looms. This is usually a more economical way to buy looms, as it's impossible to do all projects on just one type of loom. You will need different sizes and gauges of looms for different projects.

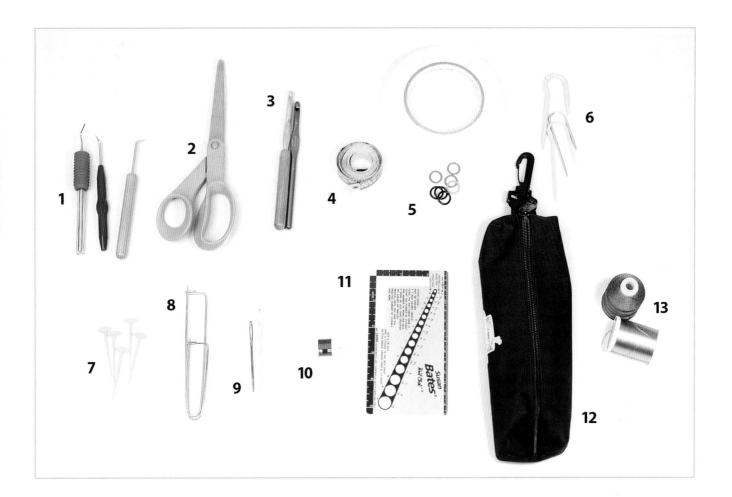

Loom Knitting Tools

Being properly equipped will go a long way toward ensuring your round loom knitting experiences are pleasurable ones!

THE ESSENTIAL TOOLS NO LOOMER CAN LIVE WITHOUT!

These are the tools every loom knitter needs to get started.

1. **The knitting tool, or pick,** is often included with your new loom. It is essential to loom knitting and it's recommended that you keep at least a few on hand, as occasionally you'll bend one or break it completely if your stitches are too tight. The knitting tool is used to work your stitches around the loom. Finding a comfortable pick is essential. The picks come with different tips; blunt picks should be used with larger pegs and heavier yarns, while those with pointed tips are meant for thinner yarns and smaller pegs. There are also knitting tools with padded handles for greater ease of use.

2. **Scissors** are an essential loomer's tool. A sharp pair of scissors will allow you to easily cut even the thickest of yarns. A small pair will be easy to take along for travel or on those days when you have a lot of appointments.

3. A **crochet hook** is needed for casting on and off the loom and picking up dropped stitches. It also can be used to weave your yarn ends into the knitting. I prefer a deep hook, as it allows me to quickly grab my yarn. One medium-size hook is all you need for loom knitting.

4. A **measuring tape** is necessary for accurate sizing of your knitting. It's also nice to have a stiff 12"/30.5 cm ruler on hand for those times when you're doing smaller projects.

5. **Stitch markers** to keep track of where you are at in the pattern.

6. **Cable needles** are used to hold your stitches or loops when making cables. They are also useful for moving stitches. They are sold in different sizes and shapes and it is recommended that you keep several on hand.

7. **Large plastic quilt pins** are used for blocking a knitted item and creating a straight seam. I don't like metal pins for blocking because they can rust and discolor your knitting. I also find metal pins too sharp; they can cut or fray your knitting.

8. **Stitch holders** look like large safety pins with a blunt end. They are useful for holding and locking stitches

How to Achieve Proper Gauge

MAKE A SWATCH! If your pattern says the gauge should be 10 sts and 14 rows = 4"/10 cm in the particular stitch used in that pattern, then cast on 10 stitches and knit 14 rows in that stitch, then bind off all the stitches (you'll learn how in Lesson 1) and measure your swatch. If it's a 4"/10 cm square, you're ready to start your pattern! If your swatch is undersized, try working your stitches more loosely; if it's oversized, try knitting with a little more tension. Not all patterns require exact gauge (loose-fitting hats, craft items), but some will (sweaters and other clothing).

Guide to Common Loom Sizes and Uses

Loom Type	Peg Spacing	Project Type	Gauge	Knitting Needle Comparison	Yarn Weights
Large gauge	$^3/_4$"/2 cm or more	Bulky weight knits	$1^1/_2$ to 2 sts per 1"/1.25 cm	US 13 (9 mm)	#5 medium worsted weight or thicker, or 2 strands #4 light worsted weight
Medium gauge	$^5/_8$"/1.5 cm, $^1/_2$"/1.25 cm, $^7/_{16}$"/11 mm	Medium weight knits	3 to $3^1/_2$ sts per 1"/1.25 cm	US 10 (6 mm)	#4 light worsted weight or thicker, or 2 strands #2 fine weight
Small gauge	$^3/_8$"/1 cm	Medium and lightweight knits	$3^1/_2$ to 4 sts per 1"/1.25 cm	US 7–8 (4.5–5 mm)	#3 or 4 light or medium worsted weight
Fine gauge	$^3/_{16}$"/5 mm	Lightweight knits	7 to 8 sts per 1"/1.25 cm	US 1–2 (2.25–2.75 mm)	#1 or 2 super fine or fine weight

for times when you have to move your stitches around quite a bit. You can also use a contrasting piece of waste yarn for this purpose.

9. **Tapestry or yarn needles** make fast work of weaving in your yarn ends at the end of a project. They have a blunt end (to keep from splitting the yarn) and larger eye for threading yarn through. They are also needed for seaming, duplicate stitch, blanket stitch, and other techniques used to enhance loom knitting.

10. A **row counter or notepad and pen** are necessary to keep track of your rows and stitches. They come in many different shapes and sizes. There are also apps for smartphones that will keep track of your stitches. I have found that I work better with a notepad and

pen—I can never seem to remember if I clicked the counter or not!

11. A **stitch guide** determines the number of stitches and rows per inch in your work for gauge. They come in plastic and metal and have ruler markings. The guide is laid on top of your knitting and allows you to count the number of stitches/rows in your knitting.

12. A **tool holder** is necessary to keep all your tools organized. It can be a fancy, store-bought sewing box or a simple plastic bag with a zip slider.

13. **Embroidery thread or floss** is needed for sewing on buttons. Regular sewing thread can be too thin and sharp for use with knitting, possibly cutting into the yarn. The thicker embroidery floss is stronger and will not damage your knitting.

A sewing basket, pom-pom makers, color wheel, and notebook are just a few extras every loom knitter can use.

HELPFUL TOOLS YOU'LL WANT IN THE FUTURE

A **yarn winder** can transform a hank or skein into a compact "cake" of yarn. These center-pull balls of yarn sit nicely and feed you the yarn smoothly while knitting; having them is particularly helpful when you are working with two strands of yarn at the same time. Storage of the cakes is easier since the cakes have flat bottoms and easily stack on one another. Yarn winders come in plastic or metal and have a wide price range. At some point, you may want a **swift** to go along with your winder. A swift holds your hank in place as you wind, keeping it tangle free.

A **sewing basket or notions holder** can make storage of all your supplies more organized. Let's face it, who doesn't like a pretty sewing basket?

A **yarn and accessory project bag** is invaluable for keeping all your project supplies in one organized space. The bags have openings at the top to feed the yarn through while knitting. Usually there is an accessory bag attached for easy transport of your supplies.

A **notebook** is a great tool for jotting down ideas and notes about patterns and yarns. One day you may want to try your hand at developing your own patterns and these notes will be invaluable to you.

A **color wheel** will help you make better decisions when combining different color yarns in one project. It shows the relationship between the primary, secondary and complementary colors and can help turn your projects from good to wow!

Pom-pom makers can make fast work of creating multiple pom-poms. They come in different sizes and are very sturdy. It is easy to make your own out of cardboard (see page 12), but these little wonders are sturdy and make a knitter's life a little easier.

Knitting needles are used for grafting the toes of socks. It is recommended that you have a couple different sizes if you like to knit socks.

The Wonderful World of Yarn

This is the truly fun part of knitting: beautiful, colorful, warm, luxurious yarn. Today, we knitters are lucky to live in a world where there is an endless supply of wool, cotton, synthetics, and blends to choose from.

It's easy to feel overwhelmed by such abundance in your local yarn shop. This chapter will help you determine

Yarn Weight Guide

Weight	0	1	2	3	4	5	6	7
Yarn type	Lace	Sock, fingering, baby	Sport, baby	DK, light worsted	Worsted, Aran, afghan	Bulky, chunky	Super bulky	Jumbo
Knit gauge in stockinette st per 1"/1.25 cm	$8^1/_4$–10 sts	7–8 sts	5–6 sts	4–5 sts	3–4 sts	2–3 sts	$1^1/_2$–2	$1^1/_2$ sts or less
Recommended knitting loom when using a single strand of yarn	Extra fine gauge	Extra fine gauge	Fine gauge	Small gauge	Medium gauge	Medium to large gauge	Large gauge	Large gauge

which yarn is best for your individual project. Taking time to learn color theory and how each yarn affects the look, feel, and utility of your project is important for great results. Always ask yourself these questions before choosing a yarn for your project:

- Who is it for?
- Does the person I'm making it for have allergies?
- Do I need the finished item to be washable or temperature-resistant?
- How much loft (the thickness of the yarn) would I like in my finished project?

To help identify the correct yarn for your project, you need to understand the characteristics of the different types of fibers available to the loom knitter.

Plant-based fibers are well known in textiles. Cotton is breathable, absorbs moisture well, and dries quickly. It is well tolerated by most people on the skin. This makes it perfect for summer knits and lightweight items. It is also machine washable, making it a good choice for everyday items. Cotton is not quite as elastic as wool and some other fibers. It's most commonly available in medium worsted weight #4 yarn, necessitating the use of two strands of yarn when using medium or large gauge looms. Organic cotton yarns are now widely available for knitters concerned about pesticide usage. Linen and bamboo are also popular choices in this category and are both durable and known for their nice drape.

Animal- or protein-based fibers are very popular with knitters. They have a rich appearance and are durable, elastic, and warm. Prices vary on these fibers depending on type and characteristics. These fibers are not always well tolerated on the skin and it's possible to be allergic to them. Sometimes wool can be quite scratchy or itchy

Raw wool before spinning; wool is washed, carded, and then spun by hand or machine into the strands that will become yarn.

on the skin, so take the time to test it on the inside of your wrist or along the sensitive neck area to see how it feels. Soaking wool in a conditioning wash like Eucalan can soften and condition the fibers, making them easier to tolerate. Animal fibers tend to hold up better if hand washed and shaped after washing. Natural fibers labeled superwash can be machine washed and do not felt. Blends with other fibers can give you the look and feel of wool, but provide greater softness and washability.

Synthetics have opened up new doors to loom knitting enthusiasts. There is now an endless array of sparkly, ruffled, sequined, and colorful yarns made for the knitter. Synthetics are manmade and usually stronger than natural fibers. They are machine washable, inexpensive, and widely available. They can contain chemicals and are nonrenewable, which can cause the fiber purist to frown upon them. Although they can be an allergen, fabrics made from synthetics are usually less scratchy than those

from animal fibers, making them a good choice for people with sensitive skin.

Another thing to consider when selecting yarn is its **thickness, or weight**. The thickness of the yarn was once determined by how many thinner, single strands (or ply) are combined to make one complete strand of yarn. To make a four-weight yarn, four single strands were combined to make that single yarn strand, making it a four-ply yarn. Today, yarn weights are not so standard. According to the Craft Yarn Council of America, there are eight weight categories of yarn, each of which should produce a predictable number of stitches per inch when using a specific needle size.

Often in loom knitting patterns you will see that two strands of yarn are called for. This is another way to affect the gauge of your knitting. As loom knitters, we can achieve a thicker fabric by adding this second strand instead of changing the yarn weight or the gauge of the

Quick Guide to Fibers

Fiber Type	Fiber Name	Description
Plant based	Egyptian cotton	Smoother and softer than other cottons, has the longest fibers.
Plant based	Pima cotton	A cross between Egyptian and American cotton.
Plant based	American cotton	Available in a wide array of colors, takes dye nicely, has medium-length fibers.
Plant based	Linen	Strong fiber, wrinkles easily.
Plant based	Bamboo	Strong fiber that creates a breathable fabric with a nice drape.
Animal based	Mohair	Luxurious, lofty, has a scratchy texture.
Animal based	Merino wool	One of the softer wools. Stronger than cotton, can pill.
Animal based	Icelandic wool	Strong fiber with a scratchy texture.
Animal based	Cashmere	Luxurious, soft, expensive.
Animal based	Alpaca	Warm, lofty, can be scratchy, expensive.
Animal based	Angora	Very soft, sheds, best used as an accent or as part of a fiber blend. Not naturally elastic. Felts easily.
Animal based	Silk	Lightweight, strong fiber with a nice sheen. Moderate to poor elasticity.
Synthetic	Nylon	Strong, elastic fiber, washes well, best in blends.
Synthetic	Acrylic	Widely available, inexpensive, machine washable, all purpose, sensitive to high heat.
Synthetic	Rayon	Inexpensive, nice sheen, highly absorbent, made from processed cellulose.

loom. To do this, hold the two strands of yarn together and knit with them as if they are one strand.

Finally, when selecting yarn for a project, we need to think about color. Solid colors are best used in patterns with intricate stitch work, like cables, as they will show up better. Light colors reflect light best and enable us to see the patterns more clearly. Dark colors will cause the pattern to recede, making it less visible. Variegated yarns can add interest to simple stitchwork, but tend to distract from more complicated stitching. Novelty yarns are also a great choice for a simple stitch pattern because they add character. When using multiple colors, grab a color wheel and decide whether you want the colors in your project to blend, complement, or contrast one another.

Finishing and Embellishing Your Knitting

Taking the time to properly finish and embellish your knits makes all the difference. Follow these steps and soon you'll be feeling confident in your skills.

Seaming

Many knitters dread projects that require seaming. I'll be honest, I love seaming knits. I think it's because I learned the proper steps early and had good results right from the start. I like the structure, shaping, and tailored look that seaming can provide.

Take the time to block your knits before seaming them together. This will make it easier to line up the seams. A large project will require careful pinning, but smaller projects may only need a couple pins to keep you on track.

MATTRESS STITCH

This stitch creates an invisible vertical seam in fabric made with stockinette stitch. Use the same yarn as in your project or a similar color.

1. Lay the two pieces side by side, right sides facing up.

2. Stretch the knitting a little and find the first row of ladder stitches near the edge of each panel.

3. Using a yarn needle, go under the first ladder stitch on one panel (back to front).

4. Now, go to the opposite panel and go under the first ladder stitch on that piece.

5. Repeat, alternating sides, until you are at the end of the piece to be seamed. Occasionally, pull gently on the working yarn and your stitches will begin to blend together and look seamless. Do not pucker your knitting by pulling too hard.

6. Finish by connecting the top two corners together, then cut the yarn if necessary and weave in the end.

In this example, the yarn has been taken under the "ladder" stitches, first on one side and then the other. For demonstration purposes, I have used a bright-colored yarn, but you will use a color that matches your knitting. Also for demonstration purposes, I have shown the technique on the second row of ladders; you will do your stitching on the first row, closer to the edge.

The ends of the yarn have been pulled gently and you can no longer see the working yarn even though it is a bright color.

GARTER STITCH SEAMING

This creates an invisible vertical seam on garter-stitched knits. Use the same yarn as in your project or a similar color.

1. Lay your two pieces side by side, right sides facing up.

2. Find the top and bottom stitches (they look like bumps) on each panel.

3. Using a yarn needle, go under the last stitch on one panel and the last stitch on the other panel.

4. Now, go back to the first panel and go under the next bottom stitch.

5. Go under the next top stitch on the other panel. This will allow the knitting to nestle neatly together.

6. Repeat, alternating panels, until you are at the top of your knitting.

7. Occasionally, pull gently on the knitting (not too hard; you don't want it to pucker), bringing it together.

8. Finish by connecting the top two corners together. Cut the yarn if necessary and weave in the end.

The working yarn has been taken first under the lower bumps in the knitting on one side, then under the top bumps on the other side. This will allow the garter stitch to nestle together once the seam is pulled snug. For demonstration purposes, the seam is being done one stitch over; you can seam closer to the edge.

The working yarn has been pulled gently and the stitches are now able to nestle together. When you use a matching yarn, your seam will now be invisible.

GRAFTING, OR KITCHENER STITCH

This technique is often used to close the toe of a sock because it does not create an uncomfortable ridge behind the seam.

1. Using a contrasting color of yarn and yarn needle, thread the needle through half the loops on your pegs and remove them from the loom. Repeat for other half of stitches. Make sure your knitting is facing in the direction you want your seam to go.

2. Place half your stitches (loops) on one regular knitting needle, keeping them in order and not twisting them. Place the remaining stitches on another needle. Hold the needles side by side in one hand.

3. Using a threaded yarn or tapestry needle, take your yarn through the first stitch on the needle closest to you, as if to purl. Then go through the first stitch on the second needle as if to knit. Keep these two stitches on the needle. This is your anchor.

4. Now take your yarn through the first stitch on the needle closest to you, as if to knit. Remove this stitch from the needle. Then go through the first stitch on the same needle as if to purl; leave this stitch on the needle.

5. Now take your needle through the first stitch on the second needle as if to purl; remove this stitch from the needle. Then go through the first stitch on the same needle as if to knit, leaving this stitch on the needle.

6. Repeat Steps 4 and 5 until there are no more stitches.

7. Pull gently to shape the stitches.

8. Fasten off and weave in the ends.

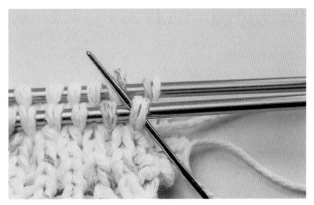

The stitches have been transferred onto the knitting needles. The needle is being taken up through the front of the stitch as if to purl.

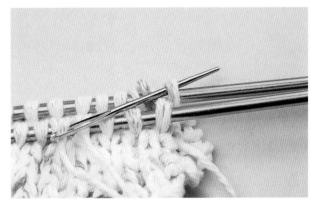

The needle is now being taken through the back of the stitch as if to knit.

Weaving in Ends

You always want to leave a 4"–5"/10–13 cm tail of yarn at the end of your knitting. To keep this tail from being unsightly, you must weave it into the back of your knitting to hide it. You can do this in two ways.

Crochet hook method: Use a crochet hook to pull the tail in and out of the knitting until the tail is completely hidden.

The crochet hook has been inserted under the stitches and is now ready to grab the end and pull it through the knitting.

Needle method: Thread it through a tapestry or yarn needle and insert it through the bumps on the back of your knitting, going in and out, until the tail is completely hidden.

The tapestry needle has been inserted under the stitches and will be pulled through the knitting, hiding the end.

Pom-Poms, Tassels, and Fringe

Pom-poms, tassels, and fringe make fun, decorative additions to hats and scarves.

POM-POMS

These can be made using one of the many pom-pom makers on the market, but it is also possible to use cardboard to make your own.

1. Cut a rectangular piece of cardboard the height of your desired pom-pom.

2. Cut two slits in the sides.

3. Lay a length of yarn across the cardboard (this is called the lifeline).

4. Wrap your yarn around the cardboard (at least 150 times for a dense pom-pom). Grab the bulk of the yarn and slide it off one side of the cardboard, being careful not to lose your tie.

5. Tie the piece of yarn in a knot, catching all the loops.

6. Cut the tops of the loops open and fluff and trim the pom-pom.

The lifeline has been cut and laid across the width of the cardboard. The yarn for the pom-pom has been wrapped around the board, top to bottom.

The yarn has been pulled off one side of the cardboard, taking care not to lose the lifeline.

Tie the lifeline yarn in a knot, making sure it is holding the yarn snug.

Cut the ends of all the loops, taking care not to cut your lifeline yarn (you will use this later to attach the pom-pom to your knitting).

The pom-pom has been been fluffed and trimmed and is now ready to use.

TASSELS

These can also be made by using cardboard.

1. Cut a piece of cardboard the length of the tassel you want.

2. Cut two slits about one third of the way down on the sides.

3. Lay a 12"/30.5 cm length of yarn across the cardboard (the lifeline).

4. Wind the yarn around the cardboard to the desired thickness.

5. Tie the front of the tassel to hold.

6. Cut the yarn at the bottom of the cardboard.

7. Take the tassel off the cardboard, being careful to keep the yarn in position. Tie the lifeline completely around the tassel.

8. Wrap the remaining lifeline around the tassel, leaving enough yarn in the back to blend in with the rest of the fringe. Trim if necessary.

The lifeline has been cut and laid across the cardboard. The cardboard is wrapped with the yarn.

When removing the tassel from the cardboard, keep the yarn in place and tie the lifeline completely around the tassel.

The lifeline has been tied around one side of the tassel.

Wrap the remaining lifeline around the tassel (where the tie is) and secure, leaving enough yarn in the back to blend in with the rest of the fringe. Trim if necessary.

Cutting the bottom of the tassel.

FRINGE

This is also made by using cardboard. Using a piece of cardboard will ensure that all your fringe is cut to the same length.

1. Cut a piece of cardboard to one half the desired length of finished fringe.

2. Wind yarn around the cardboard.

3. Cut the yarn along the bottom of the cardboard.

4. Attach one to three strands of yarn to the end of scarf or other garment with a crochet hook.

The cardboard has been wrapped with the yarn.

Cut the bottom edge of the yarn, freeing it from the cardboard.

The fringe is now ready to be added to the garment.

Fold the fringe in half. Insert the crochet hook through the knitting and grab the center of the fringe.

Pull the fringe through the knitting, leaving it on the crochet hook.

Now grab the fringe again with the crochet hook.

The fringe has now been pulled through the existing loop on the crochet hook.

Pull the fringe snug. It is now attached to your knitting.

Finishing Stitches

These stitches are both decorative and practical.

OVERCAST STITCH

Use this stitch to sew fabric or lace onto knitting or as an easy decorative edge. This stitch will hold fabric or a lining in place while allowing the knitting to still stretch a bit.

1. At the edge of your knitting, stick a needle and thread from back to front through the fabric.

2. Now go over the edge and to your left/right and come back up from back to front again through the fabric.

The needle is being taken from the back to the front of the knitting along the edge to create the overcast stitch. This stitch can be done with a tapestry needle and yarn or a regular sewing needle and thread to sew layers of fabric together.

SINGLE CROCHET

Use single crochet to put an easy decorative edge on your knitting. Although this step is always optional in loom knitting, it's advantageous to learn an easy edging for decorative purposes or to tighten up the look of a loose cast-on edge.

1. Insert a crochet hook through the first row of stitches, front to back.

2. Put the working yarn over the top of the hook (yarn over).

3. Pull the hook and yarn back up through the knitting to the front.

4. Yarn over again and pull through the two loops on your crochet hook.

5. Insert the hook through the next stitch to your left/right.

6. Repeat.

Grab the working yarn with the crochet hook and pull it up through the knitting.

Grab the working yarn again and pull it through the two stitches on the crochet hook.

The crochet hook has been inserted through the first row of stitches, front to back.

You have completed the single crochet stitch. Repeat around the edge of your garment.

BLANKET STITCH

Blanket stitch is also used to add a decorative edge to your loom knitting.

1. Bring a threaded yarn needle from the front to the back of the knitting.

2. Bring the needle around the edge and come up through the knitting to the right/left, catching the loop to form a corner.

3. Repeat along the edge.

The needle has been inserted through the front of the knitting and is being brought through the natural loop created. This stitch can be made as wide as you like.

Casting On, Knit Stitch, and Binding Off

In this lesson, I will teach you what you need to know to make your very first round loom project. It's the most basic of basics: cast on, knit, bind off.

Casting On

In round loom knitting, there are many ways to cast on (and how you do it will affect how the edge of the piece will look), but we will start with the two most popular methods: the e-wrap cast-on and the chain cast-on.

With all cast-ons, try to maintain a medium tension on the working yarn. Your stitches/wraps should be just tight enough to stay on the pegs but loose enough to pull over the pegs without struggling.

If the pattern you are following does not specify which direction you should work around the loom (clockwise or counterclockwise), then it is unimportant to the execution of the pattern and you can work in whichever direction is most comfortable for you. This is really only an issue if you are working in the round (see page 21).

E-WRAP CAST-ON

This creates a very loose edge, suitable for when you will be joining panels together. To do the e-wrap cast-on, first you need to know how a slipknot is made and how the e-wrap is done.

Making a Slipknot

To make a slipknot, make a loop at the end of your working yarn by winding the yarn once around your index finger, then pull a loop of the working end of the yarn through and pull tight on this new loop to create the slipknot. Slide it off your finger.

Wrap the working yarn around your fingers once.

Push the working yarn up through the loop created on your fingers.

Pull tight, forming the slipknot.

Making an E-Wrap (ew)

In loom knitting, the e-wrap can be used to make stitches (as in the e-wrap knit stitch), to cast on, to make lace stitches (when combined with different kinds of decreases), and to increase your stitch count at the end of a row (you'll find more about the last two in Lesson 6).

To e-wrap a peg, wind your working yarn completely around the peg, from back to front. If you are working counterclockwise around the loom, you will wrap the peg in a clockwise direction. If you are working clockwise, you will wrap the peg in a counterclockwise direction.

How to E-Wrap Cast-On

1. Place a slipknot on the holding peg or wind the yarn around the holding peg and hold.

2. Starting with the peg (peg 1) to the right or left of the holding peg, depending on the direction you will be working in, e-wrap the peg two times.

3. There will now be two wraps (loops) of yarn on peg 1; with the knitting pick, lift the bottom loop over the top loop.

4. Repeat Steps 2 and 3 for the number of pegs indicated in the pattern.

In this example, you can see the slipknot securing the yarn to the holding peg in front and the yarn being wrapped around peg 1 for the first time. The peg has been wrapped in a clockwise direction, preparing to head counterclockwise.

The yarn wrapped around peg 1 for the second time, completing Step 2.

Use the knitting tool to lift the first (bottom) wrap (loop) of yarn over the second (top) wrap (loop) of yarn.

CHAIN CAST-ON

This creates a chain edge that is tighter than the e-wrap cast-on.

1. Place a slipknot on the holding peg.

2. Position the loom so that you are working from inside the loom.

3. With a crochet hook, grab the working yarn and pull it between the first and last pegs toward the center of the loom. This creates a loop in the working yarn. With the crochet hook still in the loop, move the hook so it is now between pegs 1 and 2 and grab the working yarn.

4. Pull the working yarn through pegs 1 and 2 and through the loop on the hook.

5. Repeat Steps 2–4 for the number of pegs indicated in the pattern.

6. If you will be working in the round (see right) and the pattern states "join to work in the round," after you have cast on to your last peg, place the last loop on your crochet hook on to peg 1; you will work these two loops together as a single stitch to begin the next round.

With a crochet hook, pull the working yarn between the first and last peg to create a loop, then grab the working yarn on the outside of the loom with the hook.

Pull the working yarn through pegs 1 and 2 and through the loop on the hook. The hook is now positioned to grab the working yarn and pull it through the next loop on the hook.

Working in the Round vs. Working Flat

Knitting in the round is just what is sounds like. When you have worked the last peg around the loom, you will continue in the same direction, constantly working around the loom in rounds. Doing so will create a seamless cylinder, perfect when making garments like cowls or socks.

To work flat, when you come to the last peg of the loom, you will begin working in the opposite direction (without flipping the loom; loom knitting is always done with the right side facing out), and continue in this way, working back and forth in rows.

The Knit Stitches

There are four ways to do the knit stitch on the loom: the regular knit stitch, flat knit stitch, u-knit stitch, and e-wrap knit stitch. The first three kinds of knit stitches produce a V pattern, referred to as the stockinette stitch, and a tighter knit weave. Though they all produce the stockinette V, these knit stitches vary in tension and may be specifically called for in a pattern. For intarsia and Fair Isle, I use the regular knit stitch exclusively to ensure that the design in the fabric stands out clearly, but I prefer the flat or u-knit stitch for items that require durability (like socks) because of the tighter tension both of those stitches have. The e-wrap knit stitch creates what is known as the twisted stockinette stitch, which results in a much looser knit weave.

REGULAR KNIT STITCH (K)

This stitch is most like the knit stitch created using knitting needles.

1. Insert the knitting tool upward through the loop and grab the working yarn, keeping the working yarn to the outside of the frame.

2. Pull the working yarn down through the loop, creating a new loop.

3. Pull the loop off the peg and place the newly formed stitch on the peg.

Grab the working yarn with the pick and pull it through the existing loop on the peg to create another loop.

The knit stitch. Here you can see the V shape of this stitch.

Pull with the pick or your fingers so that the existing loop comes off the peg.

Place the working yarn above the existing loop on the peg. Insert the knitting tool up through the loop.

Place the new stitch on the peg. The knit stitch is now complete.

FLAT KNIT STITCH (FL-K)

This stitch requires practice. It is a very tight stitch and doesn't work well with yarns that do not have elasticity. It produces the tightest weave. Keep your working yarn loose and apply pressure with your thumb in between pegs to lessen the tension.

1. Push the existing loops on each peg down to the bottom of loom.

2. Position the working yarn above the loop on the peg.

3. Pull the bottom loop over the working yarn and the top of the peg.

Here you can see the existing loops pushed down to the bottom of the pegs and the working yarn positioned above the loops.

To make the flat knit stitch, you will now take the knitting pick and pull the bottom loop over the working yarn and the top of the peg.

U-KNIT STITCH (U-K)

This is an easy knit stitch to learn and produces a medium-tight stitch.

1. Lay the working yarn above the existing loop on the peg and wrap it around the back of this same peg, creating a U.

2. Pull the bottom loop over the working yarn and the top of the peg.

Here you see the U of the u-knit stitch: the working yarn wrapped around the peg above the loop.

Here the bottom loop is being pulled over the top loop, completing the u-knit stitch.

E-WRAP KNIT STITCH (EWK)

Also known as the twisted stockinette stitch, this produces the loosest weave of all the knit stitches. Most beginners learn this stitch first.

1. Working back to front, wind the working yarn around the peg.

2. Pull the bottom loop over the top loop.

A swatch of the e-wrap knit (twisted stockinette) stitch.

The peg has been e-wrapped with the working yarn.

Using the knitting pick, pull the bottom loop (for this first row or round, the bottom loop is your cast-on loop) over the top loop, completing the stitch.

Lifting Stitches

In loom knitting, you will often be asked to lift your stitches for hat brims, seaming, and stitches like the puff stitch.

LIFTING STITCHES FOR A HAT BRIM AND SEAMING

1. Reach down to the first row/round of stitches and, with the knitting pick, grab the stitch that is in line with the peg you are working on.

2. Place that stitch on the peg.

3. Treat the two loops that are now on the same peg as if they are one when you work the next round or follow the instructions for each individual pattern. Often, you will be asked to knit the bottom loop over the top loop instead.

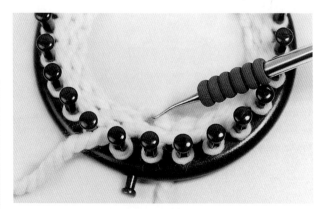

This shows the knitting pick grabbing a bottom stitch, which will be pulled up and over the peg directly above it.

LIFTING STITCHES IN THE MIDDLE OF YOUR KNITTING

1. For stitches (like the puff stitch) that require a lifted stitch, count down the number of rows/rounds specified in the pattern.

2. With your knitting tool, grab the stitch below the peg you are working on and pull that loop up onto the peg.

3. Treat the two loops that are now on that peg as if they are one when you knit or purl the next row/round.

Binding Stitches Off the Loom: The Gather Method

There are many ways to bind stitches off (BO) the loom. In this lesson, you will learn the gather method, which is very easy.

1. After finishing your last row/round, wrap the working yarn two times around the loom and cut (this ensures a nice long tail to work with).

2. Thread the end of the yarn through a tapestry or yarn needle.

3. Insert the needle down through the loop on the first peg and remove that loop from the loom; repeat for all remaining pegs.

4. Pull on the yarn gently to gather your knitting and secure by weaving in the end.

For each peg, insert the needle down through the loop.

The Perfect Red Slouchy Hat

Loom knit this trendy hat in just a few hours!

Level

Beginner

Finished Measurements

10"/25 cm from crown to brim x 21"/53 cm circumference.

Gauge

10 sts and 18 rows in pattern stitch = 4"/10 cm square

Yarn

Lion Brand Vanna's Choice, worsted weight #4 yarn (100% acrylic; 170 yd./156 m, 3.5 oz./100 g per skein)
1 skein #860-113 Scarlet

Supplies

- 41-peg (³/₄"/2 cm peg spacing) round loom
- Knitting tool
- Crochet hook
- Tapestry needle
- Tape measure or ruler

Pattern Notes

- Pattern is worked in the round.
- Pattern is worked holding two strands of the yarn and working them as one.

Slouchy Hat

Using the chain cast-on and working with two strands of yarn as a single strand, cast on to all pegs of loom; join to work in the round.

Rnds 1–15: U-knit all sts.

Lift first rnd of stitches up onto pegs, forming the hat brim. Knit bottom loops over top loops.

Rnd 16: U-knit.

Rnd 17: Ewk.

Repeat Rnds 16–17 until hat measures 10"/25 cm in length.

BO all pegs using gather method.

Fasten off. Weave in ends.

Super Soft Tube Scarf

This is an easy and elegant accent scarf.
Experiment with different colors for unlimited looks!

Level

Beginner

Finished Measurements

31"/79 cm long x 10$\frac{1}{2}$"/26.5 cm wide

Gauge

11 sts and 14 rows in twisted stockinette
(ewk) = 4"/10 cm square

Yarn

Lion Brand Jiffy Yarn, bulky weight #5 yarn
(100% acrylic; 135 yd./123 m, 3 oz./85 g
per skein)
1 skein #450-155 Silver Heather

Supplies

- 26-peg ($\frac{1}{2}$"/1.25 cm peg spacing) round loom
- Knitting tool
- Crochet hook
- Yarn needle
- Brooch, pin, or large button to embellish scarf (optional)

Pattern Notes

- Pattern is worked back and forth in rows.

Scarf

Using chain cast-on, cast on to all pegs.
Row 1: Ewk.
Repeat Row 1 until just enough yarn is left on the skein to bind off (allow two times the circumference of loom).
Working one peg at a time, reach down to first row of stitches and lift them up onto the pegs directly above them.

Thread a yarn needle with the working yarn. Insert the needle down through the top loop on peg 1, then go up through the bottom loop on peg 2, then up through top loop on peg 3, and continue in this manner to the end of the row. Do the same thing in the opposite direction until all the loops are caught on the working yarn.
Pull the loops off the loom and pull gently on the working yarn to gather the knitting.

Finishing

Weave in the ends.
If you like, place a brooch, pin, or large button in the center of gather and secure to knitting.

Another Cast-On and Bind-Off, Purl Stitch, and Knitting in Multiple Colors

I n this lesson, you will learn how to work with more than one color, a new cast-on and bind-off, and the purl stitch.

True Cable Cast-On

This is a good cast-on for loomers who would like to use the knitting tool/pick instead of a crochet hook to cast on to the loom. It looks very similar to the chain cast-on.

1. Place a slipknot on peg 1.

2. Position the working yarn above the loop on peg 1.

3. Insert the knitting pick up through the slipknot (or the last cast-on stitch), grab the working yarn, and pull it down through the slipknot (as you would in a regular knit stitch), creating a new loop.

4. Flip this loop (the top of the loop should now face downward) and place it on peg 2.

5. Repeat Steps 3 and 4 for for as many pegs as the pattern directs.

6. If you will be working in the round and the pattern states "join to work in the round," after you have cast on to your last peg, place the last loop on your crochet hook on to peg 1; you will work these two loops together as a single stitch to begin the next round.

Insert the knitting pick through the loop on the peg being worked, grab the working yarn, and pull it down through the loop on the peg.

Flip the newly formed loop (the top of the loop should now be facing downward) onto the peg next to it.

Chain 1 Bind-Off
(a.k.a. Single Crochet Bind-Off)

This bind-off creates a chain appearance along the edge of your knitting that has a moderate amount of stretch.

1. Working from the inside of the loom, transfer the loop on peg 1 to a crochet hook.

2. Grab the working yarn with the crochet hook and pull it through the loop, creating a chain 1 and binding off a stitch.

3. Transfer the loop from peg 2 to the crochet hook, then pull it through the loop already on the hook.

4. Repeat Steps 2 and 3 until all the loops have been removed from the pegs.

5. Cut the yarn and pull the end through the final loop. Weave in the end.

Grab the working yarn with the hook. You'll then pull the yarn through the loop.

Place the loop from the second peg on the crochet hook and continue repeating the steps until all the pegs are bound off.

Transfer the loop on the first peg to a crochet hook.

Purl Stitch (p)

The purl stitch is often thought of as the opposite of the knit stitch. It will make small bumps in your knitting.

1. Push the already existing loop to the top of the peg.

2. Position the working yarn so it is beneath the loop on the peg.

3. Insert the knitting pick down through the loop on the peg and grab the working yarn. Pull it through the loop on the peg to form a new loop.

4. Pull the stitch off the peg and place the newly formed loop back on the peg.

To make a purl stitch, position the working yarn beneath the loop to be worked. Insert the knitting pick down through the loop on the peg, grab the working yarn, and pull it up through the same loop, creating a new loop. Here the pick is about to grab the yarn.

To complete the purl, pull the stitch off the peg and place the new loop on the peg. Here the new loop is being put back on the peg. You can use your fingers or the pick to do this step.

Skip 1/Slip 1 (sk1/sl1)

The skip 1, or slip 1, is often used at the beginning of the row to create a neater edge. You will also see it used within a row when a stitch is to be skipped, as in lace and mosaic knitting. When asked to skip 1/slip 1, you will take your working yarn behind the peg to be skipped and position it in front of the next peg to be worked. Some stitches will require you to skip more than one peg. In this case, you would take your working yarn behind the specified number of pegs and then position it to the front of the next peg to be worked.

Here the peg at the beginning of a row has been skipped. The knitter simply ignores the first peg, going behind it, and begins the row on peg 2.

Here peg 3 is being skipped in the middle of a row by going behind it and preparing to work peg 4.

Working with Multiple Colors on the Loom

Changing colors on the loom is easy and fun! Simply secure the new color to the starter peg or an empty peg, depending on the pattern, and start knitting with it. This method will usually make a horizontal color change unless you are knitting sideways. Make sure you leave a 4"/10 cm tail for weaving in later. In most cases, you will not knot the new color to the old color (in some patterns, such as for lace, you may be called to knot your yarn to keep it from unraveling), as knotting can cause a color change where you didn't expect it or uncomfortable bumps in your knitting. You will secure the new color later when you weave in your ends. Always follow the pattern directions.

If you do not want your color change to show, always change colors on a knit row. This will give a cleaner separation between your colors. Alternately, if you would like a more casual, homemade look, as in the Mock Cable Boot Toppers (page 90), change your color on a purl row.

VERTICAL COLOR CHANGES

Adding vertical stripes to your knitting is easy with a little practice. When changing colors for vertical stripes, wind the yarns around each other once to ensure that they knit together. It's important to pull firmly on the yarns when you do this to eliminate potential gaps in your knitting.

In this photo, you see the two yarn strands being twisted around each other. This allows the two colors to link together, preventing holes in the knitted fabric.

This shows a horizontal color change on a knit row. The color change is clean, with no colors peeking through the knitting.

Here is a sample of a vertical color change. By twisting your colors together at the end of each row, you will eliminate gaps.

This is a horizontal color change on a purl row. You can see that the color change is noticeable, with the coordinating color peeking through the knitting.

FAIR ISLE

Fair Isle, also known as stranded knitting, is a technique that uses two colors in the same row, allowing the knitter to create different patterns and motifs.

Fair Isle knitting can be accomplished with either of two different methods.

1. Using the main color (MC), work all the stitches that call for that color, skipping the stitches that don't. Keep the working yarn behind the pegs that are being skipped. Once you have worked your way around the loom, drop the MC and pick up the coordinating color (CC) and work stitches that require that color. This method keeps the different colored yarns untwisted.

2. In the second method, you carry both the MC and CC together. When the pattern calls for the MC, place the CC on top of the MC, drop it, and knit with the MC. Reverse the process when using the CC to knit. This effectively twists the MC and CC together, eliminating any gaps between the colors.

In this method of Fair Isle, the different yarns are carried together. The color not being used (the blue) is placed above the other and dropped. The next stitch to be worked will be white. Doing this keeps the two yarn colors twisted together, eliminating gaps between the colors.

INTARSIA

Intarsia (also known as picture knitting) is a way to add simple details or complex designs to your work. An example of this technique is in the Christmas Stocking on page 119. For a small design, you can cut a couple yards of yarn and place it on a spool; for larger designs, you'll want to work off a ball of yarn.

To work the design, you will follow a chart, supplied in your pattern, and knit each stitch with the color indicated. You will drop the coordinating color once you are beyond the area of the actual design and not carry it along your row or round. The coordinating color will be knit back and forth just in the design area.

This is the wrong side of a design that includes both stranded knitting (the red stripes) and intarsia (the red Christmas tree). For the intarsia portion, the design is only worked in the center of the knitting and the coordinating color is not carried around the loom.

Men's Two-Way Beanie

You can loom knit this easy beanie in one evening.
Wear it as a ski cap or a slouchy hat!

Level

Beginner

Finished Measurements

11"/28 cm high (crown to edge of brim); 9"/23 cm with
   brim folded up

Gauge

10 sts and 20 rows in stockinette stitch = 4"/10 cm square

Yarn

Patons Shetland Chunky, bulky weight #5 yarn (75%
   acrylic, 25% wool; 148 yd./136 m, 3.5 oz./100 g per skein)
   1 skein #24107878042 Charcoal (MC)
   1 skein #24107878046 Oxford Grey (CC)

Supplies

- 41-peg ($^3/_4$"/2 cm peg spacing) round loom
- Knitting tool
- Crochet hook
- Tape measure

Hat

Using CC and chain cast-on, cast on to all pegs; join to
   work in the round.
Rnd 1: *K2, p2, rep from * until last peg, k1.
Cut CC and join MC.
Rnds 2–9: *K2, p2, rep from * until last peg, k1.
Rnd 10: Knit.
Repeat Rnd 10 until knitting measures 11"/28 cm.
BO all pegs using chain 1 bind-off.
Weave in ends.

Cozy
Color
Block
Infinity
Scarf

Large blocks of color make this stylish scarf a standout, and the roving yarn gives it extra cozy appeal. You can wear it doubled up as a cowl or hanging long—go with the look you like!

Level

Beginner

Finished Measurements

Approximately 57"/145 cm circumference x 8"/20.5 cm wide

Gauge

10 sts and 14 rows in twisted stockinette (ewk) = 4"/10 cm square

Yarn

Bernat Roving, bulky weight #5 yarn (80% acrylic, 20% wool; 120 yd./109 m, 3.5 oz./100 g per skein)
1 skein #16110000032 Putty (MC)
1 skein #16110000714 Coral (CC)

Supplies

- Any ³/₄"/2 cm peg spacing round loom (19 pegs used)
- Knitting tool
- Crochet hook
- Yarn needle

Pattern Notes

- The scarf is knit flat, then the ends are seamed together. If you prefer, you can leave it as a long scarf; just add 5 rows of garter stitch to the beginning and end of the scarf to keep it from curling.
- The skip 1 at the beginning of each row creates a nice, even edge.

You can also double up the scarf and wear it as a cowl.

Scarf

Using MC and chain cast-on, cast on to 19 pegs of loom.
Rows 1–30: Sk1, ewk18.
Cut MC, pick up CC.
Rows 31–60: Sk1, ewk18.
Cut CC, pick up MC.
Repeat Rows 1–60 two times.
BO all pegs using chain 1 bind-off.

Finishing

Bring ends of scarf together and seam using mattress stitch.
Weave in ends.

Knit/Purl Stitch Patterns and Creating Eyelets

Y ou can combine knits and purls to create an endless array of stitch patterns. In this chapter, I'll teach the four most commonly found in loom knitting: single rib stitch, seed stitch, double moss stitch, and garter stitch. In each case, I provide directions for flat (back and forth) knitting and knitting in the round.

Eyelets leave a hole in your knitting, which can be decorative (think lace patterns) or functional (buttonholes).

Single Rib Stitch

This is a reversible, no-curl stitch, often used on cuffs, collars, and sweater bands—anywhere a snug but stretchable fabric is desired. Note: The instructions given here are for a single rib, but you can easily adapt the number of knits and purls for a wider rib (i.e., k2, p2).

FLAT PANEL KNITTING (MULTIPLE OF 2 STS)

Row 1: *K1, p1, rep from * to end.
Row 2: *P1, k1, rep from * to end.
Repeat Rows 1 and 2 for pattern.

KNITTING IN THE ROUND (MULTIPLE OF 2 STS)

Rnd 1: *K1, p1, rep from * to end.
Repeat Rnd 1 for pattern.

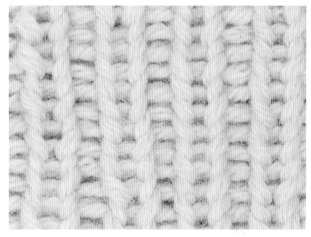

Single rib stitch. The Vs are knit stitches; the bars are the purl stitches.

Seed Stitch

This is a reversible, no-curl stitch with lots of texture.

FLAT PANEL KNITTING (MULTIPLE OF 2 STS WORKED OVER 2 ROWS)

Row 1: *K1, p1, rep from * to end.
Row 2: *K1, p1, rep from * to end.
Repeat Rows 1 and 2 for pattern.

KNITTING IN THE ROUND (MULTIPLE OF 2 STS WORKED OVER 2 RNDS)

Rnd 1: *K1, p1, rep from * to end.
Rnd 2: *P1, k1, rep from * to end.
Repeat Rows 1 and 2 for pattern.

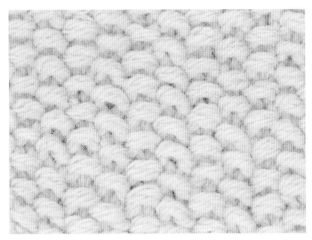

Seed stitch.

Double Moss Stitch

This is a reversible, no-curl, textured stitch.

FLAT PANEL KNITTING (MULTIPLE OF 4 STS WORKED OVER 4 ROWS)

Rows 1 and 4: *K1, p1, rep from * to end.
Rows 2 and 3: *P1, k1, rep from * to end.
Repeat Rows 1–4 for pattern.

KNITTING IN THE ROUND (MULTIPLE OF 4 STS WORKED OVER 4 RNDS)

Rnds 1 and 2: *K1, p1, rep from * to end of rnd.
Rnds 3 and 4: *P1, k1, rep from * to end of rnd.
Repeat Rnds 1–4 for pattern.

Double moss stitch.

Garter Stitch

This is a reversible, no-curl stitch, great for scarves where both sides will show. It is the same whether you are knitting flat or in the round.
Row/Rnd 1: Knit.
Row/Rnd 2: Purl.
Repeat Rows/Rnds 1 and 2 for pattern.

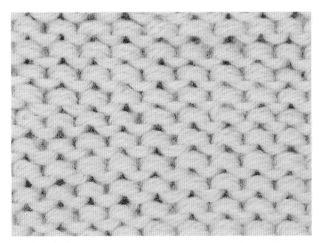

Garter stitch.

Eyelets and Buttonholes
(Yo-k2tog/Yo-p2tog)

Eyelets and buttonholes are made the same way on the knitting loom. Both leave a hole within your knitting. Sometimes it's for utility reasons, as for a buttonhole, and other times it's for decorative purposes, like creating eyelets or a lacy pattern. You can make these using knit or purl stitches.

1. Lift the stitch/loop from peg 1 and place it on peg 2.

2. Bring the working yarn in front of peg 1 and lay it across this peg, creating the yarn over (yo).

3. Knit (k2tog) or purl (p2tog) both stitches/loops on peg 2 as one. On the next row/round, knit the yarn over as you would any other stitch.

The stitch/loop from peg 1 has been moved to peg 2.

The working yarn is now positioned in front of peg 1 (creating the yarn over) and is ready to be knit or purled on peg 2.

Important Note

THROUGHOUT THIS BOOK, peg 1 is always the next peg to be worked, no matter what direction you are working in. Also, when asked to knit/purl 2 stitches or loops as one, you will do this by treating both loops as if they were one loop and knit/purl them as you normally would. ■

Here you can see two stitches being knit (k), as one, together.

Here you can see two stitches being purled (p), as one, together. The stitches are done exactly the same as if there were only one stitch.

Easy Wine Bottle Cozy

You'll want to work up a stock of these cute and quick twisted stockinette and rib stitch wine bottle covers. They make a great hostess gift paired with a nice bottle of wine. Combine different yarn colors and embellishments for endless looks from the same easy pattern!

Level

Beginner

Finished Measurements

12"–13"/30.5–33 cm high x 10"/25 cm circumference

Gauge

11 sts and 16 rows in twisted stockinette (ewk) = 4"/10 cm square

Yarn

Patons Shetland Chunky, bulky weight #5 yarn (75% acrylic, 25% wool; 148 yd./136 m, 3.5 oz./100 g per skein) 1 skein Country Sky Variegated (MC)
Small amount of contrasting yarn for top of bottle and pom-poms (CC)

Supplies

- 24-peg (³/₄"/2 cm peg spacing) round loom
- Knitting tool
- Crochet hook
- Yarn or tapestry needle
- 2 buttons, any size (optional)

Pattern Notes

- This pattern is worked in the round counterclockwise.
- The cozy has a round of eyelets at the neck to run a tie through. The directions below include making pom-poms to attach to it, but you can also just weave a pretty ribbon and tie in a bow or make a braid from yarn, as show in the photo.

Bottle Cozy

BODY

Using MC and chain cast-on, cast on to all pegs; join to work in the round.
Rnds 1 and 3: Knit.
Rnds 2 and 4: Purl.
Rnd 5: Ewk.
Repeat Rnd 5 until knitting measures 9"/23 cm or the height at which your bottle begins to narrow for the neck. (This measure works for tall wine bottles. You can change this measure to make it work for whatever height bottle you have.)

NECK

Rnd 1: *K2, yo-k2tog, rep from * to end of rnd.
Rnds 2–15: *K1, p1, rep from * to end of rnd.
Cut MC, pick up CC.
Rnd 16: Knit.
Rnd 17: Purl.
Rnd 18: Knit.
BO all sts using chain 1 bind-off.

Finishing

Weave in all ends.
Thread a piece of yarn 2"/5 cm longer than the bottom of wine cozy through the eyelets. Make two small pom-poms (see page 12), leaving a tail on both for tying onto the yarn.
Tie pom-poms to ends of yarn already woven onto wine cozy. Tie yarn in a bow.
Attach two buttons to the front center of the cozy, if you like.

So Soft Basket-Weave Cowl

A combination of natural fibers gives this cowl an elegant look. It's a quick and easy loom-knitting project and another example of how knit and purl stitches can be combined to create attractive patterns—in this case, the basket-weave effect at the front of the cowl!

Level

Beginner

Finished Measurements

10"/25 cm high x 21$\frac{1}{2}$"/55 cm around

Gauge

10 sts and 12 rows in twisted stockinette (ewk) = 4"/10 cm square

Yarn

Brown Sheep Company Lamb's Pride, bulky weight #5 yarn (85% wool, 15% mohair; 125 yd./114 m, 4 oz./113 g per skein)
1 skein #M11 White Frost (MC)
Lion Brand Fisherman's Wool, medium worsted weight #4 yarn (100% wool; 465 yd./425 m, 8 oz./227 g per skein)
1 skein #150-098 Natural (CC)

Supplies

- 31-peg or more ($\frac{1}{2}$"/1.25 cm or $\frac{5}{8}$"/1.5 cm peg spacing) round loom (31 pegs used)
- Knitting tool
- Crochet hook
- 4 brown medium buttons

Pattern Notes

- Pattern is worked as a flat panel, starting left to right. It is then seamed together.
- You will work with a single strand of MC and two strands of CC.

Cowl

Using MC and chain cast-on, cast on to 31 pegs of the loom.
Using two strands of CC, place a slipknot on holding peg of loom.
Row 1: *Ewk 1 with CC, ewk 1 with MC, rep from * to end.
Repeat Row 1 until knitting measures 17"/43 cm.
Cut CC.

FRONT SECTION

Row 1: Ewk.
Row 2: *Ewk4, p4, rep from * until last 3 pegs, p3.
Row 3: P3, *ewk4, p4, rep from * to end.
Rows 4–7: Repeat Rows 2 and 3 two times.
Row 8: *P4, ewk4, rep from * until last 3 pegs, ewk3.
Row 9: Ewk3, *p4, ewk4, rep from * to end.
Rows 10–14: Repeat Rows 8 and 9 two times.
Row 15: *Ewk4, p4, rep from * until last 3 pegs, p3.
Row 16: P3, *ewk4, p4, rep from * to end.
Rows 17–20: Repeat Rows 15 and 16 two times.
BO all sts with chain 1 bind-off.

Finishing

Seam ends together using mattress stitch.
Sew buttons on every other center block.
Weave in ends.

Working around the Loom and the Three-Stitch I-Cord

I f you really want to get creative, it's important to learn how to work around your loom. Knowing how to work in sections on the loom will enable you to do braids, hat brims, earflaps, hats with flat tops, and many other things. You can easily go from flat panel knitting to knitting in the round and back again.

In this project (the Two-Way Braided Scarf, see page 55), three different sections (in different colors) are being worked on the loom at the same time. To braid the sections, you simply slide each section onto separate stitch holders (after achieving the appropriate length), braid them, and then place each section back onto the loom in the new braided sequence.

Working Sections on the Loom

There are various different techniques you can employ to work the loom in sections.

In this example, five stitches have been moved onto a stitch holder. The stitches can now be moved to a new position on the loom.

THE PARTIAL BIND-OFF AND CAST-ON

Sometimes it will be necessary to cast on or off a portion of the loom while leaving the other stitches on, as is the case with the neck strap for the baby bib pattern on page 124. When doing this, the pattern will tell you how many stitches/pegs to bind off (for example, BO9), and it might also tell you what kind of bind-off to use. Bind off as directed, which will leave you with a loop on your crochet hook. Place that loop on the next peg and then work the two loops on that peg as one as directed by the pattern.

A partial cast-on is done in a similar fashion. You will cast on the number of pegs indicated and place your last loop on the next peg to be worked (if it's in the middle of a row/round) or onto the last peg (if it's at the end of a row). Those loops will be worked as one stitch. This type of cast-on is most often done between sections, such as earflaps. Partial cast-ons can also be done in patterns where more than a two-stitch increase is called for at the end of a row (more dramatic, less gradual increases). In that case, your last loop would be placed on the last peg in the row.

In this example, the pattern indicated to BO4. The loomer has bound off 4 pegs and is preparing to put the last loop onto peg 5. The two loops on peg 5 will then be worked as if they were one.

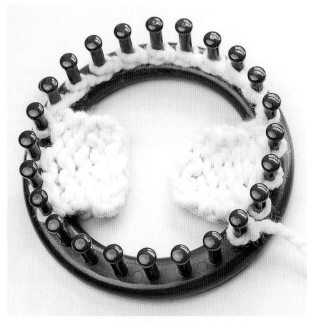

In this example, one section has been knit on the left (the first 5 pegs), 8 pegs have been cast on (in between the two sections), and another section has been knit on the right (the last 5 pegs). Always use the same cast-on method as your foundation row unless otherwise stated in the pattern.

WORKING SHORT ROWS ON THE LOOM

Often within loom knitting patterns you will be asked to work in short rows. When this is called for, the peg numbers to be worked will always be specified in the pattern. Ignore all other pegs in the row but the ones indicated and work them for the specified number of rows, changing direction at the end of each row. Sometimes a wrap and turn (see page 59 for the tutorial) will be called for (as in the Christmas Stocking, page 119), but not always (as in the Turban-Style Headband, page 81).

USING STITCH MARKERS

Stitch markers are a loomer's best friends. They will keep you on the right track, particularly when stitch patterns become more complicated and/or when you are working sections of the loom, and will greatly increase the accuracy and speed of your knitting. The types of things that can be used as stitch markers include: multicolor plastic stitch markers, small rubber bands, metal and rubber washers, and art tape.

Every knitter develops their own favorite method for keeping track of their stitches. Mine, by far, is to use white art tape. I can place a small piece on the loom at the base of the peg I want to mark and it leaves no residue on the loom. Then I can write on it, indicating knit, purl, and so on, freeing me from having to memorize the sequence or constantly having to reference the written pattern. The tape also does not get in the way when I'm trying to lift my stitches off the pegs. Unfortunately, depending on what the loom is made of, tape does not always stick to the base, so it is not always an option. I recommend trying different markers and seeing which is the best fit for you.

Here is a loom set up with colored stitch markers. For this particular project, the black markers are being used to indicate knit stitches, the green markers for purls, and the purple markers for where a cable twist will be worked.

Three-Stitch I-Cord

This I-cord can be worked in any direction on the loom. The peg nearest your working yarn becomes peg 1. Any of the knit stitches can be used to make an I-cord. Try experimenting to see which ones work best for you.

Using a chain or e-wrap cast-on, cast on to 3 pegs.

1. Knit peg 1.

2. Position working yarn behind peg 2; knit peg 3.

3. Knit peg 2.

4. Repeat Steps 1–3, pulling gently downward on the knitting, until the desired length is reached.

In this example, 3 pegs have been cast on. Peg 1 is now being knit using the e-wrap knit stitch. The knitter will next be ready to knit peg 3 and then peg 2.

ADDING A TAPER TO THE END OF AN I-CORD

1. Move the stitch on peg 1 to peg 2, knit both stitches as one.

2. Move the stitch on peg 3 to peg 2, knit both stitches as one.

3. Bind off.

A finished three-stitch I-cord with a tapered end.

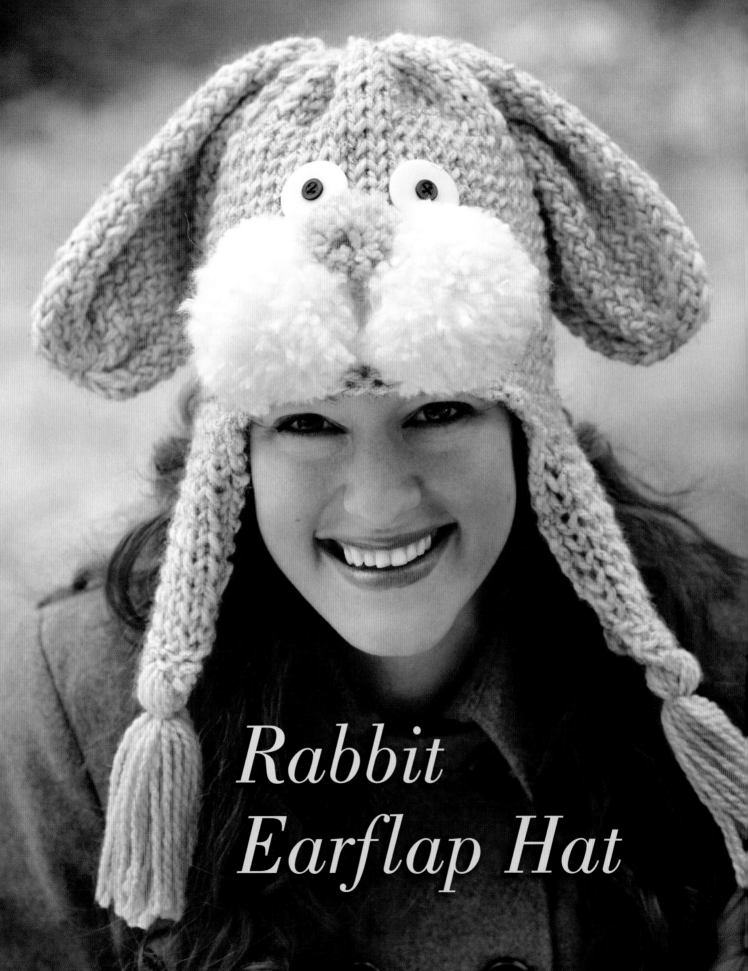

Rabbit Earflap Hat

This bunny hat is perfect for the fun-loving teen or adult. It's sure to put a smile on your face while keeping you warm this winter!

Level

Confident beginner

Finished Measurements

Crown to brim: $7^3/4$"/19.5 cm
Earflaps: 6"/15.25 cm long
Rabbit ears: $8^1/2$"/21.5 cm long

Gauge

10 sts and 12 rows twisted stockinette (ewk) = 4"/10 cm square

Yarn

Lion Brand Wool-Ease Chunky, bulky weight #5 yarn (80% acrylic, 20% wool; 153 yd./140 m, 5 oz./140 g per skein)
1 skein #630-402 Wheat (MC)
Premier Yarns Deborah Norville Serenity Baby, medium worsted weight #4 yarn (100% acrylic; 175 yd./160 m, 3.5 oz./100 g per skein)
1 skein #5004 Pastel Pink (CC1)
Patons Divine, bulky weight #5 yarn (79.5% acrylic, 18% mohair, 2.5% polyester; 142 yd./130 m, 3.5 oz./100 g per skein)
1 skein #06006 White Icicle (CC2)

Supplies

- 48-peg ($^5/_8$"/1.5 cm peg spacing) round loom
- 24-peg ($^5/_8$"/1.5 cm peg spacing) round loom
- Knitting tool
- Crochet hook
- Stitch markers or white art tape
- 4"/10 cm pom-pom maker and 1"/2.5 cm pom-pom maker
- 4 buttons: 2 white (large), 2 black (small)

Pattern Notes

- The earflaps are worked first, one at a time, in rows, then the stitches for the hat are cast on in between the flaps, attaching the flaps directly to the hat.
- The main body of the hat is worked in the round counterclockwise.
- When asked to wrap a peg, you will do the same e-wrap used in the e-wrap knit stitch, without knitting the peg (see Lesson 1, page 19).
- The rabbit ears are worked separately on the smaller loom, then sewn onto the hat.
- Tassels that are 6"/15.25 cm long can be sewn to the bottom of earflaps if desired (shown, see page 52; see page 13 for a tutorial), or three-stitch I-cord ties can be added to the bottom of the earflaps in place of tassels if desired (not shown). Just follow the directions in this lesson and make them as long as you like!

Hat

MAKE FIRST EARFLAP

Mark pegs 8, 18, 31, and 41. You will be knitting the earflaps between these markers.
Using the 48-peg loom, MC, and chain cast-on, cast on to pegs 11–15.
Row 1: Ewk5.
Row 2: E-wrap peg 10; do not knit. Purl pegs 11–15. E-wrap peg 16; do not knit.
Row 3: K7 (all pegs, including e-wrapped pegs).
Row 4: P7.
Row 5: E-wrap peg 17; do not knit. Ewk7. E-wrap peg 9; do not knit.
Row 6: Starting with peg 9, p1, k7, p1.
Row 7: P1, ewk7, p1.
Row 8: E-wrap peg 8; do not knit. P1, k7, p1. E-wrap peg 18; do not knit.
Row 9: Starting with peg 18, ewk1, p1, ewk7, p1, ewk1.
Even-numbered rows 10–24: K1, p1, k7, p1, k1.
Odd-numbered rows 11–23: Ewk1, p1, ewk7, p1, ewk1.
Row 25: Ewk1, p1, ewk7, p1, ewk1, wrap pegs 7 and 6.

Row 26: K3, p1, k7, p1, k1.
Using chain cast-on, cast on to pegs 19 and 20.
Row 27: Ewk15
Cut MC, leaving a 5"/12.5 cm tail.

MAKE SECOND EARFLAP

Using MC and chain cast-on, cast on to pegs 34–38.
Row 1: Ewk5.
Row 2: E-wrap peg 33; do not knit. Purl pegs 34–38. E-wrap peg 39.
Row 3: K7.
Row 4: P7.
Row 5: E-wrap peg 40; do not knit. Ewk7. E-wrap peg 32; do not knit.
Row 6: Starting with peg 32, p1, k7, p1.
Row 7: P1, ewk7, p1.
Row 8: E-wrap peg 31; do not knit. P1, k7, p1. E-wrap peg 41; do not knit.
Row 9: Starting with peg 41, ewk1, p1, ewk7, p1, ewk1.
Even-numbered rows 10–24: K1, p1, k7, p1, k1.
Odd-numbered rows 11–23: Ewk1, p1, ewk7, p1, ewk1.
Row 25: Ewk1, p1, ewk7, p1, ewk1, e-wrap pegs 30 and 29; do not knit.
Row 26: Starting with peg 29, k3, p1, k7, p1, k1.
Using chain cast-on, cast on to pegs 42 and 43.
Row 27: Ewk15.
Cut MC.

BODY OF HAT

Foundation rnd: Using MC and chain cast-on, cast on to pegs 1–5, k15, cast on to pegs 21–28, k15, cast on to pegs 44–48. Join to work in the round.
Rnd 2: K5, ewk15, k8, ewk15, k5.
Rnd 3: P5, k15, p8, k15, p5.
Rnd 4: Ewk.
Rnd 5: Knit.
Repeat Rnds 4–5 until hat measures 7¹/₂"/19 cm.
BO all sts using gather method.
Weave in ends.

RABBIT EARS (MAKE 2)

Using the 24-peg loom, MC, and chain cast-on, cast on to 14 pegs. Starting with peg 14, chain cast on pegs 14–24 with CC1; join to work in the round.
Rnd 1: Ewk, working 14 pegs of MC, then 10 pegs of CC1. When you switch colors, twist the two strands around one another; this will eliminate any gap between the two colors.
Repeat Rnd 1 until knitting measures 7"/18 cm in length. Cut CC1. Tie MC and CC1 together.
BO all sts using MC and gather method.
Tie the two yarn tails at the bottom of your knitting together, making sure the pink side creases inward, creating the ear shape.
Sew ears onto top of hat.

Create the Face

Make two large pom-poms using CC2 and sew them onto the bottom front of hat for the rabbit's cheeks. Make one small pom-pom using CC1 and sew it between and just above the two larger pom-poms for the nose.
Take a long length of yarn and weave it through all three pom-poms with a yarn needle, securing them together. Make sure yarn does not show in the front. This will bind the three pom-poms together.
Place the smaller button on top of the larger button and sew onto the face. Repeat for second eye.

Two-Way
Braided
Scarf

This versatile scarf can be worn straight or buttoned as an infinity scarf. It looks complicated but is surprisingly easy!

Level

Confident Beginner

Finished Measurements

56"/142 cm long x 6^1/$_2$"/16.5 cm wide

Gauge

12 sts and 18 rows in garter stitch = 4"/10 cm square

Yarn

Plymouth Encore Mega, super bulky weight #6 yarn (75% acrylic, 25% wool; 64 yd./58.5 m, 3.5 oz./100 g per skein)
  2 skeins #0999 (burgundy; MC)
  1 skein #0217 (black; CC1)
  1 skein #0146 (cream; CC2)

Supplies

- Any loom with ^{5}/$_8$"/1.5 cm peg spacing (using 15 pegs)
- Knitting tool
- Crochet hook
- Measuring tape
- 3 large buttons
- Stitch markers

Pattern Notes

- Pattern is worked flat, starting left to right. There are three color sections that are worked at the same time (without twisting the yarns, so as to keep them separate), then taken off, braided, and returned to the pegs to secure and add a second border.
- There is a row of eyelets along one end of the scarf, for buttonholes.

Scarf

BORDER

Place stitch markers on pegs 5 and 10.
Using MC and chain cast-on, cast on to 15 pegs.
Odd-numbered rows 1–9: Ewk.
Even-numbered rows 2–10: Purl.

BRAID SECTIONS

Place a slipknot of CC1 on peg 6.
Place a slipknot of CC2 on peg 11.
Row 1: Ewk, working pegs 1–5 in MC, pegs 6–10 in CC1, and pegs 11–15 in CC2. Do not wrap the colors around one another as you change yarns; you want the sections to remain separate.
Row 2: Purl, working in each color as you come to it.
Repeat Rows 1 and 2 until total knitting measures 55"/140 cm; end knitting on Row 2.
Cut working yarn on all sections, leaving a 6"/15.25 cm tail for each.
Lay your knitting flat and braid the three sections until you reach the end.
Note: Your knitting should lay flat even after braiding and not be so tight that it starts to fold.
Place the stitches from each section back on the loom in their new order; take care not to twist the stitches as you put them back on the pegs.

SECOND BORDER

Join MC.
Rows 1, 3, and 5: Ewk.
Rows 2 and 4: Purl.
Row 6: P2, yo-p2tog, p3, yo-p2tog, p3, yo-p2tog, p1.
Rows 7 and 9: Ewk.
Rows 8 and 10: Purl.
BO all sts using chain 1 bind-off.

Finishing

Weave in all ends.
Line up the buttons along the border on one side with the eyelets on the other side and sew to secure.

The Wrap and Turn and Another Knit Stitch

In this lesson, you will learn how to wrap and turn. The wrap and turn, often abbreviated w&t, is the most common way of creating short rows within your knitting. By wrapping the yarn around an adjacent peg without knitting it and then knitting back the other way, the loom knitter can prevent holes from forming in the finished fabric. We will also learn the double e-wrap knit stitch, which is a fun way to create an open weave without lifting stitches!

Wrap & Turn (w&t)

The wrap and turn, also known as short-row shaping (though there are additional methods of short-row shaping), allows you to gradually shorten or lengthen your rows. This technique is usually seen in patterns for socks, but can also be used for all kinds of shaping and to make hat brims, and it creates a soft, curving edge. It can be done in the middle of a row or at the end.

1. Knit or purl to where the w&t is called for; take the stitch off the next peg, and hold it with your knitting tool or fingers.

2. Wrap the working yarn around the now-empty peg, wrapping from the back to the front of the peg.

3. Place the stitch on your knitting tool back on the peg.

4. With the working yarn, knit or purl back in the opposite direction without knitting the peg you did the

w&t on. You will work those two stitches as one on the next row.

Note: The wrap and turn can also be done by eliminating Step 1 and placing the wrap above the already existing loop on the peg; this is best done on the edge of a garment and not within the knitting (to avoid gaps), as with socks and similar items.

The stitch has been taken off the peg where the w&t is called for (Step 1). For demonstration purposes, this is being shown at the end of a row, but it is done the same way if the w&t is called for in the middle of a row.

The working yarn has been wrapped once around the peg from back to front (Step 2).

The stitch being held on the knitting tool has been placed back on the peg (Step 3).

You are now ready to work back in the opposite direction; do not work the stitches on the peg you just did the w&t on.

Double E-Wrap Knit Stitch
(d-ewk)

This stitch is achieved by doing the e-wrap stitch two times on the same peg. It creates an open, loose stitch.

1. E-wrap the peg.

2. Pull the bottom loop over the top loop (ewk).

3. Repeat Steps 1 and 2, then move to the next peg.

E-wrap the peg, back to front.

Pull bottom loop/stitch over top stitch and peg. Repeat these two steps to complete the double e-wrap knit stitch.

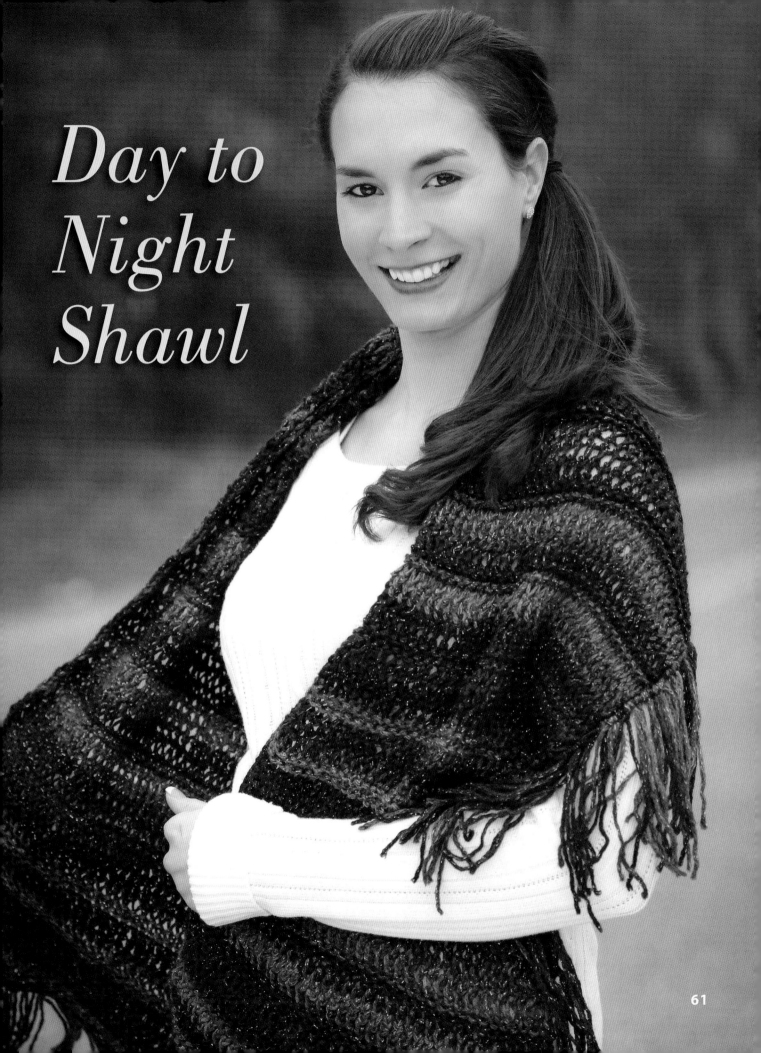

Day to Night Shawl

Perfect for day or night, this lacy rectangular shawl has a touch of shimmer. It can be worn over the shoulders, belted, snug around the neck, or as a hood and scarf in one. The lace effect is achieved with no complicated lifting of the stitches using the double e-wrap knit stitch, which produces a loose weave.

Level

Confident Beginner

Finished Measurements

60"/152.5 cm across x 16"/40.5 cm deep (without fringe)

Gauge

Not necessary; use measuring tape to achieve proper size.

Yarn

Red Heart Boutique Midnight, light worsted weight #4 yarn (65% acrylic, 23% wool, 6% nylon, 6% metallic; 153 yd./140 m, 2.5 oz./70 g per skein)
    4 skeins #E786-1953 Nightfall

Supplies

- 41-peg (^{3}/$_4$"/2 cm peg spacing) round loom
- Knitting tool
- Crochet hook
- Yarn needle

Pattern Notes

- Pattern is worked as a flat panel, starting left to right.

The shawl is long enough that you can wear it belted.

Left: Or you can drape it over your head and wrap the ends for a hooded scarf effect.

Right: Or arrange it loosely around your neck.

Shawl

Using chain cast-on, cast on to all pegs; do not join to work in the round.

Row 1: Knit.

Row 2: Purl.

Rows 3–6: K1, p1, d-ewk37, p1, k1.

Row 7: K1, p1, k37, p1, k1.

Row 8: K1, p1, p37, p1, k1.

Row 9: K1, p1, k37, p1, k1.

Row 10: K1, p1, p37, p1, k1.

Repeat Rows 3–10 until knitting measures 60"/152.5 cm; finish your knitting on Row 9.

BO all sts using chain 1 bind-off.

Weave in ends.

Finishing

Add 6³/₄"/17.5 cm (finished measurement) long fringe (see page 15) to three sides of shawl, one strand per stitch.

Comfy Slipper Socks

Level

Intermediate

Sizes

Women's small (6–8), medium (8–9), and
large (9–10)

Finished Measurements

12 (13$^1/_2$, 15)"/30.5 (34, 38) cm length,
9"/23 cm circumference for all sizes
(knitting stretches to 14")

Gauge

13 sts and 22 rows in stockinette stitch =
4"/10 cm square

Yarn

Premier Yarns Deborah Norville Serenity
Chunky Heathers, bulky weight #5 yarn
(100% acrylic; 109 yd./100 m, 3.5 oz./100
g per skein)
1 skein #0001 Smokey (MC)
Premier Yarns Deborah Norville Serenity
Baby, medium worsted weight #4 yarn
(100% acrylic; 175 yd./160 m, 3.5 oz./
100 g per skein)
1 skein #5001 White (CC)

Supplies

* 24-peg ($^5/_8$"/1.5 cm peg spacing) round loom
* Knitting tool
* Crochet hook
* Measuring tape
* Yarn needle
* Small pom-pom maker (optional)

*These cozy slipper socks are textured on the top of the foot
but have a simple knit stitch on the bottom that
keeps them comfortable when you walk.*

Pattern Notes

* You need only a small amount of CC but you will work a
  double strand of it. You could buy two skeins or wind a
  single skein into two balls to pull from.
* The socks are worked counterclockwise on all pegs
  in the round to the top of the heel. At that point you
  switch to back-and-forth knitting, using the wrap & turn,
  over just 12 pegs to shape the heel. When the heel is
  complete, you will go back to knitting in the round on
  all pegs to complete the foot and toe. The toe end will
  be grafted together.
* It is recommended that you measure as you knit for
  proper fit.

Sock (make 2)

CUFF

Using two strands of CC and chain cast-on, cast on to all pegs; join to work in the round.

Rnd 1: Knit.
Rnd 2: Purl.
Cut CC and change to one strand MC.
Rnds 3 and 4: Knit.
Rnd 5: *K1, p1, rep from * to end.
Rnd 6: Knit.
Rnds 7–18: Repeat [Rows 3–6] 4 (5, 6) times.

START HEEL

You will be working in short rows over 12 pegs, changing direction at the end of each row.

Row 1: K11, w&t peg 12.
Row 2: K10, w&t peg 1.
Row 3: K9, w&t peg 11.
Row 4: K8, w&t peg 2.
Row 5: K7, w&t peg 10.
Row 6: K8, w&t peg 1.
Row 7: K9, w&t peg 11.
Row 8: K10, w&t peg 24.
The heel is finished.

BEGIN FOOT

Work in the round again, on all pegs.
Rnds 1 and 2: Knit.
Rnd 3: K12, *k1, p1, rep from * to end.
Rnd 4: Knit.
Repeat [Rnds 1–4] 10 (11, 12) times.

BEGIN TOE

Cut MC. Change to two strands CC.
Rnds 1, 3, 5, and 7: Knit.
Rnds 2, 4, and 6: K12, p12.

Finishing

Graft toe of sock closed using Kitchener stitch (see tutorial on page 11) or seam if desired.
If you like, make two 1"/2.5 cm pom-poms (see tutorial on page 12) and attach to front of sock.

Increasing, Decreasing, and Openwork on the Loom

In this lesson, you will learn how to increase and decrease your stitches on the round loom. This is the basis for all shaping, lace, and other openwork in knitting. You will also learn how to do the double crochet bind-off.

Increasing

Increasing (or adding stitches) allows the loom knitter to make a panel wider. It is commonly used to shape items that fan out, such as triangle scarves, sleeves, and stuffed animals.

MAKE 1 (M1)

This type of increase is done within the row, so as to maintain a nice, neat edge.

1. Move the last stitch worked in your row to the next empty peg.

2. Reach below to the ladder stitch beneath the empty peg; lift this stitch and twist it.

3. Place the newly formed stitch onto the empty peg.

4. Work the next row as instructed in the pattern.

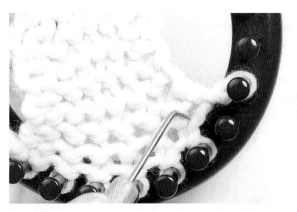

For an M1 increase, move the last stitch worked in the row to the next peg, leaving an empty peg. The knitting pick is about to pull up the ladder stitch between the two pegs.

Pull up the ladder and twist it, as shown here. The next step is to place it on the empty peg in front of it.

CASTING ON (CO)

While often thought of as providing the foundation row of stitches for a piece, you can also cast on to pegs to increase the number of stitches in a row. The cast-on will be done exactly the same way as your foundation row but only on the particular pegs specified in the pattern using the cast-on method indicated; if none is specified, then use the cast-on method used for the foundation row. You will often see this done on items such as visor and earflap hats (like the rabbit hat on page 52). You can use it for a single-stitch increase, but it's more frequently used when increases of more than two stitches are needed. This type of increase produces a less gradual increase to your row.

WRAPPING PEGS

This type of increase always takes place at the end of a row. It uses the basic e-wrap that you learned in Lesson 1.

1. Knit to the end of the row.

2. E-wrap the specified number of empty pegs at the end of the row (usually no more than two). Turn and begin working the next row as instructed. The last wrapped peg will now be your new peg 1 for the next row.

In this example, the two pegs at the end of the row have been e-wrapped, increasing the row by two stitches. The knitter is now ready to turn and start the next row working the newly formed stitches.

Decreasing

Decreasing the number of stitches on the loom allows you to make a panel narrower. For a nice, smooth edge, it's best to decrease one or two stitches in from the edge. Below are two of the most common ways to decrease. They are mirror images of one another and can be used in pairs or individually.

K2TOG OR P2TOG

In my patterns, a k2tog (knit 2 together)/p2tog (purl 2 together) creates a right or left slanting decrease depending on which direction you are knitting. It is most often done at the beginning of a row and will slant in the same direction you have moved your stitches.

1. Move the stitch from peg 1 to peg 2.

2. Move all previous stitches on that row inward to fill the empty peg; be sure to keep the stitches in their original order.

3. Work the two stitches now on peg 2 as one (as directed in pattern).

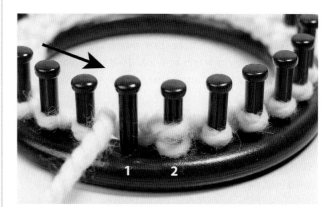

In preparation for the k2tog/p2tog, the stitch from peg 1 has been moved to peg 2 and placed on top of the stitch already on that peg.

SSK/SSP

The ssk/ssp (or slip slip knit/purl) also creates a left or right slanting decrease, depending on which direction you are knitting. It is the mirror image of the k2tog. It is most often done near the end of a row. The ssk/ssp will also slant in the direction your stitches were moved.

1. Move the stitch from peg 2 to peg 1.

2. Move all stitches (towards the end of the row) inward to fill the empty peg; be sure to keep the stitches in their original order.

3. Work both stitches on peg 1 as one (as directed by the pattern).

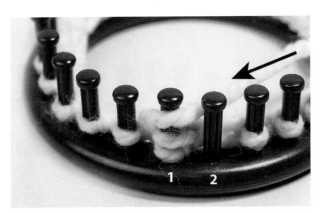

In preparation for the ssk, the stitch from peg 2 has been moved to peg 1 and placed on top of the stitch already on that peg. The working yarn has been laid above the two stitches in preparation for the knit stitch. If the pattern called for a purl, the working yarn would be below the two loops/stitches.

Lace and Openwork Stitches

Now that you understand increases and decreases, you are ready to loom knit lace. Lace is lovely and delicate and often even the simplest lace stitches look intricate.

EW-K2TOG/EW-P2TOG

An ew-k2tog/p2tog (e-wrap around empty peg, knit/purl 2 together) is often used in lace or openwork and can also be used to make eyelets. It is similar to the k2tog except that you will wrap the empty peg instead of moving your stitches inward to fill the empty peg. You may also choose to eliminate Steps 1 and 3 and not place one stitch beneath the other. If your pattern does not specify, you are free to experiment with the two methods.

1. Lift the stitch from peg 2 and hold it with your fingers or a cable needle.

2. Move the stitch from peg 1 to peg 2.

3. Place the stitch you are holding back onto peg 2.

4. E-wrap the empty peg (peg 1), bringing the yarn to the front of peg 2.

5. Work the two stitches on peg 2 as one, as directed.

Ew-k2tog/p2tog: The stitch from peg 1 has been placed onto peg 2 and the working yarn has been wrapped around the empty peg 1. Peg 2 is now ready to be worked. In this example, the peg is ready to be knit.

EW-SSK/SSP

This ew-ssk/ssp (e-wrap empty peg, slip slip knit/purl) can be done in two ways; either follow all steps or eliminate Steps 1 and 3 unless a particular method is called for in a pattern.

1. Lift the stitch from peg 1 and hold it with your fingers or a cable needle.

2. Move the stitch from peg 2 to peg 1.

3. Place the stitch you are holding back onto peg 1.

4. Work the two stitches on peg 1 (as one) as directed.

5. E-wrap the empty peg.

The stitch from peg 2 has been moved to peg 1.

CHAIN 2 BIND-OFF

This bind-off method is used when you need a medium stretch on your edge.

1. Place stitch on peg 1 onto a crochet hook.

2. Grab the working yarn and pull through the stitch (creating a chain 1).

3. Grab the working yarn again and pull through that loop (creating a chain 2).

4. Place the stitch from peg 2 onto the crochet hook and pull it through the loop on the crochet hook.

5. Repeat Steps 2–4 until all the pegs have been bound off.

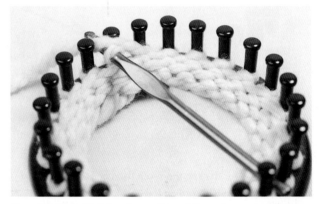

Here the first stitch has been slipped from the peg onto the crochet hook and the working yarn is being grabbed to pull through the stitch for the chain 1.

So Stylish Leg Warmers

A fresh take on the leg warmer!
This project makes use of the chain 2 bind-off.

Level

Beginner

Finished Measurements

11"/28 cm high; fits up to 15"/38 cm calf.

Gauge

13 sts and 28 rows in stockinette stitch = 4"/10 cm square

Yarn

Lion Brand Jiffy, bulky weight #5 yarn (100% acrylic;
    135 yd./123 m, 3 oz./85 g per skein)
    2 skeins #450-153 Black

Supplies

- 36-peg (¹/₂"/1.25 cm peg spacing) round loom
- Knitting tool
- Crochet hook
- Measuring tape
- Optional: decorative buttons

Pattern Notes

- For wider calves, I recommend you use a loom with ¹/₂"/1.25 cm peg spacing but with more pegs than called for here; 3 pegs give you approximately 1"/2.5 cm extra width; work as a flat panel and seam closed if it is not possible to get a loom with the number of pegs you need.

Leg Warmers (make 2)

Using chain cast-on, cast on to all pegs; join to work in the round.
Rnds 1–13: *Ewk2, p2, rep from * to end.
Rnds 14–56: U-knit.
Rnds 57–69: *Ewk2, p2, rep from * to end.
BO all sts using chain 2 bind-off.
Weave in ends. Add buttons if desired.

Waterlily Lace Triangle Scarf

Soft and bright, this versatile scarf can be worn as a shawl, off the shoulder, or wrapped snug around your neck!

Level

Intermediate+

Finished Measurements

58"/147 cm along top edge; 20"/51 cm deep

Gauge

1 st and 16 rows in pattern stitch = 4"/10 cm square

Yarn

Premier Yarns Spice Shop, super bulky weight #6 yarn (50% acrylic, 41% cotton, 9% polyester; 79 yd./72 m, 2.8 oz./80 g per skein)
2 skeins Cool Waters

Supplies

- 41-peg (³/₄"/2 cm peg spacing) round loom
- Knitting tool
- Crochet hook
- Yarn needle

Pattern Notes

- Scarf is knit sideways in a flat panel, starting left to right, and utilizes peg wrapping at the end of the rows to increase and k2tog's to decrease, building the triangular shape.
- Knit the last peg on k2tog/ssk rows.

Scarf

Using chain cast-on, cast on to 3 pegs.
Row 1: K1, ew-k2tog, k1.
Row 2: Ewk to end. Wrap next empty peg.
Row 3: *K1, ew-ssk, rep from * to end.
Row 4: Ewk to end. Wrap next empty peg.
Row 5: *K1, ew-k2tog, rep from * to end.
Repeat Rows 2–5 until all pegs on loom have stitches on them.
Repeat Rows 2 –3.
Next row: K2tog, *ew-k2tog, k1, rep from * to end.
Next row: Ewk.
Next row: K2tog, *ew-ssk, k1, rep from * to end.
Next row: Ewk.
Repeat last four rows until there is only one peg with a stitch.
BO using chain 1 bind-off.

Finishing

Weave in ends.
Block scarf if desired.
Make fringe to measure 6¹/₂"/16.5 cm (see page 15). Attach it in clusters of five strands, 2³/₄"/5 cm apart, on two sides (do not attach fringe on top edge).

Fabulous Felt, Putting in a Lining, and Getting Your Curl On

In this lesson, you will learn about felting. Felting is fun and easy, and it transforms your loom knitting into a completely different kind of fabric. You will also be given a quick lesson in how to add a lining to a handbag or tote, as these are both great candidates for felting. Also, you'll learn why knitting curls and how to incorporate that curl into your design or eliminate it in your projects.

Felting

Felting is the process of matting together wool or other animal fibers. These types of fibers have little barbs that, when exposed to hot water and pressure or agitation, will latch onto one another and fuse together in a smooth fabric. Once a fiber is felted, it cannot be reversed.

Felting is not an exact science; some trial and error should be expected. Your knit item will shrink considerably in the process, so it must be knit much larger than what you want the final dimensions to be. There is no need for complicated stitch work when felting, as you will not be able to see stitch definition once the felting process is complete. A simple stockinette or garter stitch is fine.

100% wool before felting. In this example, you can see the stitch definition before felting.

The same wool after felting. Most of the stitch definition is gone after just one felting cycle.

Tips for Felting

- Most mistakes in your knitting will not show once the item is felted.
- Do not use fibers that say "superwash." They will not felt even if they are made of natural fibers.
- Even though acrylics don't felt, you can judiciously work them together with natural fibers that do to create cool effects.
- It's a good idea to knit a swatch of the yarn you intend to felt and do a test run to see how your machine and the yarn felt.
- You don't need a washing machine to felt. You can felt entirely in the dryer! Hand wash your item, blot or carefully squeeze most of the water out of it, place in a lingerie bag, and put in your dryer along with an old towel or a couple of old tennis balls. Run it on high heat and check your item every ten minutes until you achieve the desired effect.
- You can partially felt an item, leaving it with some stitch definition. This is particularly useful if your item is shrinking too much.
- Your item will be one of a kind. No two items felt the same.

Here are the steps for felting your loom knitting:

1. If you are using a front-loading washing machine, soak the item to be felted in hot water until thoroughly saturated. This will help to speed up the felting process. This step is not necessary with a top-loading machine.

2. Place your item in a lingerie bag or pillowcase. This will protect the washing machine from becoming clogged with lint.

3. Set the washer for a hot wash/cold rinse on the shortest cycle possible. Add a mild clothes detergent. If you have hard water, try adding a little baking soda. Add an old towel or a couple of tennis balls (in a pillowcase to keep fibers out of your knitting) into the washing machine to amplify the agitation.

4. If you have a top-loading machine, check on the progress of your knitting frequently. This will not be possible with a front loader, hence setting it for the shortest cycle possible on your machine.

5. When your item is almost entirely felted (it will look like a solid piece, with very little stitch definition), you can put it in the dryer to finish the felting process. Rewet the item first if it's been through the spin cycle. Check on the item every ten minutes until the item reaches the desired size and degree of felting.

Note: You are using the heat/tumble motion of the dryer to continue the felting process; you do not want your item to dry in the dryer (keep wetting if necessary).

6. Now air-dry the piece. If your item needs to have a particular shape, you must block it or shape it *before* it dries. Once the item dries, it will maintain its shape forever and can't be reversed. Pin it to a blocking board or stuff it with plastic bags until you achieve proper shape.

Adding a Fabric Lining to a Felted Bag

Although it is not necessary to line a felted bag, it can enhance its look and utility. Use a coordinating color or a richly patterned fabric to play against the color of the bag.

1. Measure your bag's height and width; add $^1/_2$"/1.25 cm seam allowance.

2. Cut two pieces of fabric using those measurements.

3. With wrong sides together, measure 1"/2.5 cm from the right bottom corner and make a mark on the bottom and side seam; connect the two markings by drawing a straight line. Cut along this line with scissors; repeat on left side.

4. Seam the sides and bottom together, leaving top open.

5. Fold the top down $^1/_2$"/1.25 cm; iron flat.

6. Pin the lining to the inside of the bag so the top of the lining is about $^1/_4$"/.75 cm down from the top of the bag.

7. Hand sew along the top edge as close to the edge as possible.

Cut two pieces of fabric to those measurements and seam the sides and bottom together.

Pin the lining to the inside of the bag so it is $^1/_4$"/6.5 mm from the top of the bag.

Measure the height and width of the bag to be lined; add $^1/_2$"/1.25 cm to each measure for seam allowance.

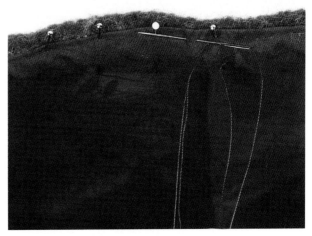

Stitch the top of the lining to the bag.

Why Is My Knitting Curling?

This is a common question beginning loom knitters ask. You will see a significant amount of curling on loom-knitted panels that will later be seamed together—as is the case with the messenger bag pattern in this lesson—particularly in pieces knit in one type of stitch such as stockinette. This happens because the front side of the knitting is all knits and the back side all purls; these two stitches are not the same size, which creates tension in the fabric and causes it to curl.

Here you can see how a swatch knit in a single stitch will curl (this has been worked in twisted stockinette).

What can you do about this? The answer is, not much. If you block the knitting, it will only be a temporary fix. The best solution is to avoid it completely or use it to your advantage. You can avoid it by making sure your edges start with an equal combination of stitches, knits and purls. This is why you will often see a border around blankets, scarves, and sweater bands. Usually a type of ribbing is used, but garter stitch works well too.

You can also use the inclination to curl to your advantage, as I have in the headband pattern in this lesson. Although a combination of stitches was used, the numbers of each stitch are not equal, resulting in mild curling, giving it a unique look. The coral and gray infinity scarf in Lesson 2 is worked in twisted stockinette, resulting in some curling, which was somewhat minimized by seaming the ends together, but it is also part of the look of the scarf. Slight or significant curling can also benefit a nonreversible piece where you don't want the wrong side to be visible, as the piece will curl in on itself.

Felted
Messenger
Bag

This unisex messenger bag is perfect for all the gadgets in your life!

Level

Beginner

Finished Measurements

12"/30.5 cm high x 13"/33 cm wide, after felting

Gauge

Not necessary; item will be felted.

Yarn

Patons Classic Wool Worsted, medium worsted weight #4 yarn (100% wool; 210 yd./192 m, 3.5 oz./100 g per skein)
3 skeins #00224 Grey Mix (MC)
1 skein #00230 Bright Red (CC)

Supplies

- 41-peg (³/₄"/2 cm peg spacing) round loom
- Knitting tool
- Crochet hook
- Measuring tape
- Two 1"/2.5 cm D-rings
- 2 small leather belts with holes in the leather
- 2 carabiners

Pattern Notes

- Project is worked holding two strands of yarn and working them as one.
- Panels are worked flat; do not join to work in the round.

Messenger Bag

FRONT PANEL

Using two strands CC and chain cast-on, cast on to all pegs; do not join to work in the round.

Rows 1–23: Ewk.
Cut CC. Change to two strands MC.
Rows 24–51: Ewk.
Row 52: Purl.
Row 53: Ewk.
Repeat Rows 52 and 53.
BO all sts using chain 1 bind-off.

BACK PANEL

Using two strands MC and chain cast-on, cast on to all pegs; do not join to work in the round.
Rows 1–74: Ewk.
Row 75: Purl.
Row 76: Ewk.
Repeat Rows 75 and 76.
BO all sts using chain 1 bind-off.

BOTTOM OF BAG

Using two strands MC and chain cast-on, cast on to 35 pegs.
Rows 1–13: Ewk.
BO all sts using chain 1 bind-off.

Assemble the Bag

Weave in all ends. Using the mattress stitch, seam the front of the bag to the back of the bag, then the bottom of the bag to the top of the bag. Sew the D-rings onto the bag, centering them above the side seams.

Now felt the bag, shape, and dry completely.

With a needle and embroidery thread, sew belt onto center of the bag by seaming at the bottom of the flap, the top of the bag, and bottom of the bag. (Tip: Use a hammer and thin nail to make holes in the leather for seaming.) Cut away excess leather. Use second belt as shoulder strap, using carabiners to attach belt to D-rings.

Turban-Style Headband

Headbands are perfect quick loom-knitting projects! Mild curling and a textured stitch (called the fleck stitch) give this one a unique look.

Level

Confident Beginner

Finished Measurements

4^1/$_2$"/11.5 cm wide x 20"/51 cm circumference

Gauge

14 sts and 22 rows in pattern stitch = 4"/10 cm square

Yarn

Brown Sheep Company Lamb's Pride Bulky (85% wool, 15% mohair; 125 yd./114 m, 3.5 oz./100 g per skein) 1 skein #M11 White Frost

Supplies

- 48-peg (^{1}/$_2$"/1.25 cm peg spacing) round loom
- Knitting tool
- Crochet hook
- Stitch holder or contrasting color length of waste yarn

Pattern Notes

- Pattern is worked flat, starting left to right, then seamed together at the end.
- The first stitch of each row is skipped to maintain a nice, even edge.
- You will be working this headband in sections (similar to the braided scarf on page 55). This will allow you to change your stitch positioning.

Headband

FIRST SECTION

Using chain cast-on, cast on to 14 pegs.
Rows 1 and 2: Sk1, k13.
Row 3: Sk1, *k1, p1, k1, rep from * to end.
Row 4: Sk1, k13.
Repeat [Rows 1–4] 11 times.
Next two rows: Sk1, k13.

SECOND SECTION

Now begin working in short rows, working pegs 14–8 only.
Row 1: Sk1, *k1, p1, k1, rep from * to end.
Rows 2–4: Sk1, k6.
Repeat [Rows 1–4] 6 times.
Next row: Sk1, *k1, p1, k1, rep from * to end.
Next row: Sk1, k6.
Cut working yarn.
Now begin working in short rows using pegs 1–7. Repeat instructions for pegs 14–8.
Take a stitch holder or piece of contrasting color yarn and a yarn needle and thread it through the loops on pegs 14–7. Keep the stitches in order and don't let them twist.
Remove the stitches from the pegs, cross over the other knitted section, and place the stitches on pegs 42–48.

THIRD SECTION

You will now knit in long rows again over pegs 42–7.
Rows 1 and 2: Sk1, k13.
Row 3: Sk1, *k1, p1, k1, repeat from * to end.
Row 4: Sk1, k13.
Repeat [Rows 1–4] 11 times.
Next two rows: Sk1, k13.
BO all sts using chain 1 bind-off.

Finishing

Weave in all ends
Seam the ends together. Block the headband if desired.

Twisting Stitches: Mock Cables

Often referred to as mock cables, the left and right twist are usually a loom knitter's first attempt at knitting cables. Making cables in knitting requires crossing one group of stitches over another, taking them out of their original order, creating cables. This cabling technique is easy and results in a narrow cable over just two stitches/pegs.

Make this easier on yourself by putting small pieces of white art tape beneath the pegs that are to be twisted. Place an arrow on the tape beneath the peg whose stitch you will put on the stitch holder and you won't have to remember which stitch goes on the peg last.

Left Twist (LTW)

1. Place the stitch from peg 1 on a stitch holder.

2. Pick up the stitch on peg 2 with your knitting tool and put it on peg 1.

3. Transfer the stitch on the holder to peg 2.

4. Knit both pegs. Left twist completed.

The stitch from peg 1 on a stitch holder.

The stitch from peg 2 has been moved to peg 1.

The stitch from the stitch holder has been placed on peg 2. The stitch holder can now be removed.

Both stitches (on pegs 1 and 2) can now be knit. In the photo, the stitch on peg 1 is in the process of being knit.

Twist/Cable Tips

- On the row before the twist is called for, knit the pegs that you will be twisting extra loose to allow for easier moving.
- Lighter colored yarns provide better stitch definition, allowing your twists to stand out.
- Twists (and cables) cause your knitting to narrow horizontally, so you need to add extra pegs to allow for this shrinkage. For example, you may want to use a size larger hat loom if you plan to add several cables to your knitting. This is accounted for in written patterns.
- When knitting cables, you do not have to cross your stitches on every row. You will knit several plain rows in between the turning rows; just be sure to keep the number of rows the same. ■

Right Twist (RTW)

1. Place the stitch from peg 2 on a stitch holder.

2. Pick up the stitch on peg 1 with your knitting tool and put it on peg 2.

3. Transfer the stitch on the holder to peg 1.

4. Knit both pegs. Right twist completed.

Here you can see a sample of the right and left twists completed.

Extra Stretchy Bind-Off

This bind-off is a perfect choice for those items knit in the round that will need extra stretch, such as boot toppers and close-fitting items that will be pulled over your head. Normally, a bind-off is never as flexible or stretchy as a cast-on, but this one provides almost an identical amount of stretch. It is easy to do with a little practice.

Here you see Step 3. The knitter is taking the needle down through the stitch on peg 1. The arrow indicates Step 4; this is the previous stitch that you will take your needle (up) through.

1. Wrap your working yarn three times around the loom and cut.

2. Thread the end of the yarn through a tapestry needle.

3. Insert the needle down through the stitch on the first peg. Do not remove the stitches from the pegs until Step 7.

4. Insert the needle up through the stitch on the previous peg.

5. Take your working yarn behind the first peg and go to the second peg. Take your needle down through the stitch on the second peg.

6. Repeat Steps 3–5 all the way around the loom, finishing on peg 1.

7. Remove the stitches from the pegs and weave in end.

Baby Bear
Spa Robe

This spa-quality robe has a soft, thick, luxurious feel when finished. Baby will love to snuggle into it after bath time or before bed!

Level

Intermediate+

Sizes

Newborn (6 months, 12 months)

Finished Measurements

Length (shoulder to hemline): 15 (16, 17)"/38 (40.5, 43) cm
Sleeve (armpit to cuff): 4 (5, 6)"/10 (12.5, 15.25) cm
Chest (armpit to armpit): 9 (10, 11)"/23 (25.5, 28) cm

Gauge

10 sts and 10 rows in twisted stockinette (ewk) = 4"/10 cm square

Yarn

Bernat Baby Blanket Yarn, super bulky weight #6 yarn (100% polyester; 72 yd./65 m, 3.5 oz./100 g per skein)
4 skeins #16110303202 Baby Blue

Supplies

- 48-peg (⅝"/1.5 cm peg spacing) round loom
- Knitting tool
- Crochet hook
- 4 buttons (Velcro or snaps can also be used)
- Embroidery thread and regular needle

Pattern Notes

- Pattern is worked in nine flat sections, each section started working left to right. The sections are then sewn together.
- There are buttonholes on the belt and robe.
- It is recommended you make the robe larger to allow for growth.

Robe

BACK PANEL

Using chain or crochet cast-on, cast on to 24 (26, 28) pegs.
Rows 1, 3, 5, and 7: U-knit.
Rows 2, 4, and 6: Purl.
Row 8: Ewk.
Row 9: U-knit.
Repeat [Rows 8 and 9] 33 (35, 37) times.
BO all sts with chain 1 bind-off.
Weave in ends.

FRONT RIGHT PANEL

Using chain cast-on, cast on to 12 (13, 14) pegs.
Rows 1, 3, 5, and 7: U-knit.
Rows 2, 4, and 6: Purl.
Row 8: Ewk.
Row 9: U-knit.
Repeat [Rows 8 and 9] 33 (35, 37) times.
BO all sts using chain 1 bind-off.
Weave in ends.

FRONT LEFT PANEL

Using chain cast-on, cast on to 16 (17, 18) pegs.
Rows 1, 3, 5, and 7: U-knit.
Rows 2, 4, and 6: Purl.
Row 8: Ewk11 (12, 13), p1, ewk2, p1, ewk1.
Row 9: U-k1, p1, u-k2, p1, u-k11 (12, 13).
Row 10: Ewk11 (12, 13), p1, RTW, p1, ewk1.
Row 11: U-k1, p1, u-k2, p1, u-k11 (12, 13).
Rows 12–39: Repeat [Rows 8–11] 6 (6, 7) times.
Row 40: Ewk11 (12, 13), p1, ewk2, yo, k2tog.
Skip to Rows 44–63 for newborn size only, BO after Row 63.
Row 41: Repeat Row 9.
Row 42: Repeat Row 10.
Row 43: Repeat Row 11.
Rows 44–63: Repeat [Rows 8–11] 5 times.
Rows 64–67: Repeat Rows 40–43.
Rows 68–79: Repeat [Rows 8–11] 3 times.

Row 80: Ewk -,(12, 13), p5.
Row 81: U-knit.
Row 82: Ewk -, (12, 13), p3, yo, p2tog.
Row 83: U-knit.
BO all sts using chain 1 bind-off.
Weave in ends.

SLEEVES (MAKE 2)

Using chain cast-on, cast on to 22 (23, 25) pegs.
Rows 1, 3, 5, and 7: U-knit.
Rows 2, 4, and 6: Purl.
Row 8: Ewk.
Row 9: U-knit.
Rep [Rows 8–9] 8 (10, 12) times.
BO all sts using chain 1 bind-off.
Weave in ends.

HOOD

Using chain cast-on, cast on to 30 (32, 34) pegs.
Rows 1, 3, 5, and 7: U-knit.
Rows 2, 4, and 6: Purl.
Row 8: Ewk.
Row 9: U-knit.
Repeat Rows 8 and 9 until hood measures 8 (8, 9)"/20.5
    (20.5, 23) cm.
BO all sts using chain 1 bind-off.
Weave in ends.

BELT

Using chain cast-on, cast on to 5 pegs.
Row 1: Sk1, u-knit to end.
Row 2: Sk1, ewk to end.
Repeat Rows 1 and 2 until belt measures 17 (18, 20)"/43
    (45.75, 51) cm.
Next row: Sk1, ewk1, yo-k2tog, ewk1.
Next row: Sk1, u-knit to end.

Next row: Sk1, ewk to end.
Next row: Sk1, u-knit to end.
Next row: Sk1, ewk1, yo-k2tog, ewk1.
Next row: Sk1, u-knit to end.
Next row: Sk1, ewk to end.
Next row: Move stitch on peg 1 to peg 2 and stitch on peg 5 to peg 4. U-knit all pegs.
Next row: Move stitch on peg 1 to peg 2 and u-knit. Move stitch on peg 3 to peg 2 and u-knit.
BO all sts using chain 1 bind-off.
Weave in ends.

BEAR EARS (MAKE 2)

Using chain cast-on, cast on to 7 pegs.
Row 1: Ewk.
Row 2: U-knit.
Repeat [Rows 1 and 2] 9 times.
Next row: Move stitch on peg 1 to peg 2 and stitch on peg 7 to peg 6, u-knit all pegs
Next row: Ewk.
Next row: Move stitch on peg 1 to peg 2 and stitch on peg 5 to peg 4, u-knit all pegs.
Next row: U-knit.
BO all sts using chain 1 bind-off.
Weave in ends.

Assembly

All seams are done using the mattress stitch.
With right sides facing out, sew front right panel to back panel. You will seam 2"/5 cm from where sleeve will attach at shoulder. Repeat for left front panel.
Mark center of each sleeve by folding in half widthwise and marking with a pin. Line this pin up with shoulder seam, then mattress stitch sleeve to front and back panels, leaving long side of sleeve open. Repeat on other side for second sleeve.
Now seam the long side of the sleeve from cuff to armpit. Be sure to pin in place to make sure seams stay aligned.
Fold hood in half lengthwise to mark center of hood and align with center back; seam together. Now seam together the top of the hood.
Mark center of back panel 8"/20.5 cm above hemline. Mark center of belt. Attach belt to robe with several stitches at the back. Bottom of belt should be 8"/20.5 cm above hemline or where you desire.
Sew large button on end of belt. Belt has two buttonholes.
Sew three buttons on front of robe, aligning with buttonholes.
Sew on bear ears.
Weave in all ends.

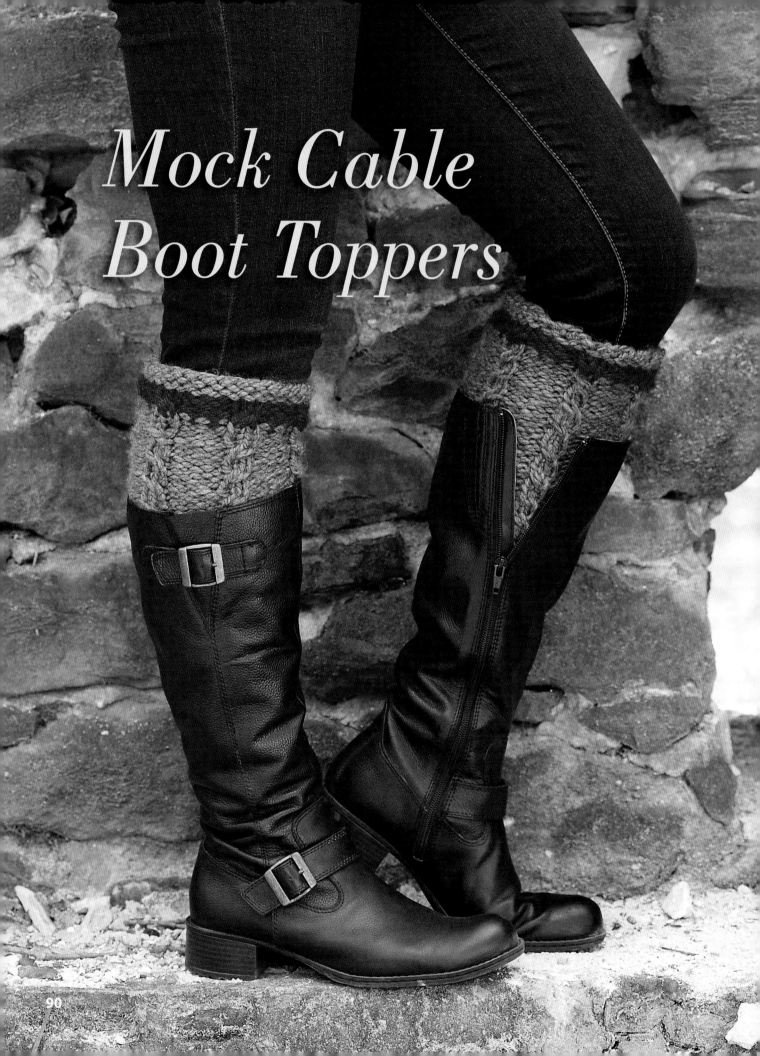

Mock Cable Boot Toppers

These boot cuffs are both functional and stylish. They fit nice and deep into your boots for extra warmth and a smooth fit. Mock cables are quick to knit and add beautiful texture to your knitting.

Level

Intermediate

Finished Measurements

8"/20.5 cm circumference; stretches to fit up to 18"/45.75 cm calf

Gauge

10 sts and 18 rows in pattern stitch= 4"/10 cm square

Yarn

Premier Yarns Deborah Norville Chunky Heathers, bulky weight #5 yarn (100% acrylic; 109 yd./100 m, 3.5 oz./ 100 g per skein)
  2 skeins #0001 Smokey (MC)
Lion Brand Hometown USA, super bulky weight #6 yarn (100% acrylic; 81 yd./113 m, 5 oz./142 g per skein)
  1 skein #135-114 Tampa Spice (CC)

Supplies

- 31-peg ($^{11}/_{16}$"/1.75 cm peg spacing) round loom
- Knitting tool
- Crochet hook
- Yarn needle

Pattern Notes

- Toppers are worked in the round.

Toppers (make 2)

Using chain cast-on, cast on to all pegs; join to work in the round.
Rnd 1: Knit.
Rnd 2: Purl.
Rnds 3, 4, and 6: *P3, k2, rep from * to last peg, p1.
Rnd 5: *P3, RTW, rep from * to last peg, p1.
Rnds 7–30: Repeat [Rnds 3–6] 6 times.
Cut MC. Change to CC.
Rnds 31–34: Rep Rows 3–6.
Cut CC. Change to MC.
Rnd 35: Knit.
Rnd 36: Purl.
Rnd 37: Knit.
BO all sts using extra-stretchy bind-off.
Weave in ends.

Your First Cables!

Now that you've mastered the twist, let's move on to cables! Honestly, they're not difficult, they just take a bit of dexterity. Believe me, the results are well worth the effort! In this chapter, you'll learn the two most common cables, worked over four pegs and over six pegs, crossing right and crossing left.

You will need a cable needle (which has a deep bend to secure the stitches and points on each end so that you are able to slip the stitches back on the pegs in the order in which you slipped them onto the cable holder). Be careful that you put the stitches back onto the pegs in the right order. When doing all cables, I like to use a cable needle for each of the stitches that gets pulled off so I don't forget which stitch needs to be moved first. Experiment with both methods to see which way works best for you! Stitch markers are also helpful for keeping track of your cable stitches.

An important tip when working cables is to keep the tension loose on your knitting so you don't have to tug at the stitches when transferring them from the stitch holder to different pegs. In particular, try to knit loosely where you will be cabling on the row or round before.

4-Peg Cable Stitches

4-STITCH RIGHT CROSS (4-ST RC)

1. Place the stitches from pegs 1 and 2 onto a cable needle and position it to the inside of the loom, behind the pegs.

2. Knit peg 3; then, with the knitting tool, move the stitch to peg 1, being careful not to twist it.

3. Knit peg 4, then move it to peg 2.

4. Transfer the stitch from peg 1 being held on the cable needle to peg 3; knit it.

5. Transfer the stitch from peg 2 being held on the cable needle to peg 4; knit it.

6. Pull gently on all the stitches to tighten and even them out.

The stitches have been taken from pegs 1 and 2 and put onto individual cable needles. Be sure to position the cable needle(s) behind the pegs.

The stitch on peg 3 has been knit and moved to peg 1.

The stitch on peg 4 has been knit and moved to peg 2.

The stitch from peg 1 (on the cable needle) has been moved to peg 3.

The stitch from peg 2 (on the cable needle) has been moved to peg 4.

4-STITCH LEFT CROSS (4-ST LC)

1. Skip pegs 1 and 2. Knit the stitches on pegs 3 and 4.

2. Place the stitches from pegs 3 and 4 onto a cable needle and position it in the center of the loom, behind the pegs.

3. Knit the stitch on peg 1, then knit the stitch on peg 2.

4. Move the stitch from peg 2 to peg 4. Move the stitch from peg 1 to peg 3.

5. Transfer the stitch from peg 3 being held on the cable needle to peg 1. Transfer the stitch from peg 4 being held on the cable needle to peg 2.

6. Pull gently on all the stitches to tighen and even them out.

The stitch from peg 2 has been moved to peg 4.

Pegs 1 and 2 have been skipped and peg 3 is being knit.

The stitch from peg 1 has been moved to peg 3.

The stitches from pegs 3 and 4 have been placed on the cable needles.

The stitches from the cable needle have been moved to pegs 1 and 2.

6-Peg Cable Stitches

These cables are worked in the same way as the 4-peg cable stitches, except you will cross three stitches instead of two, yielding a wider cable. You will be stretching your stitches a lot so it is recommended that you use a yarn with elasticity when including these cables. Wool is a good choice for large cables.

Here is an example of the 6-stitch cable.

6-STITCH RIGHT CROSS (6-ST RC)

1. Slip the stitches from pegs 1, 2, and 3 onto a cable needle and position in the center of the loom, behind the pegs.

2. Knit peg 4; move it to peg 1.

3. Knit peg 5; move it to peg 2.

4. Knit peg 6; move it to peg 3.

5. Transfer the stitch from peg 1 being held on the cable needle to peg 4; knit it.

6. Transfer the stitch from peg 2 being held on the cable needle to peg 5; knit it.

7. Transfer the stitch from peg 4 being held on the cable needle to peg 6; knit it.

8. Gently pull on all stitches to tighten and even them out.

6-STITCH LEFT CROSS (6-ST LC)

1. Skip pegs 1, 2, and 3, positioning the working yarn behind them.

2. Knit pegs 4, 5, and 6; place those stitches onto a cable needle and position it in the center of loom, behind the pegs.

3. Knit pegs 1, 2, and 3.

4. Move stitch from peg 3 to peg 6.

5. Move stitch from peg 2 to peg 5.

6. Move stitch from peg 1 to peg 4.

7. Transfer the stitches from pegs 4, 5, and 6 being held on the cable needle to pegs 1, 2, and 3 in that order.

8. Gently pull on the stitches to tighten and even them out.

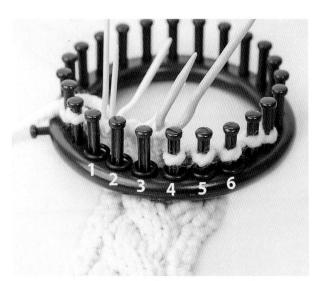

Here you see Step 1 of the 6-stitch cable and a sample of the resulting cable stitch coming off the loom. I often use an individual cable needle for each stitch, as shown in this photo.

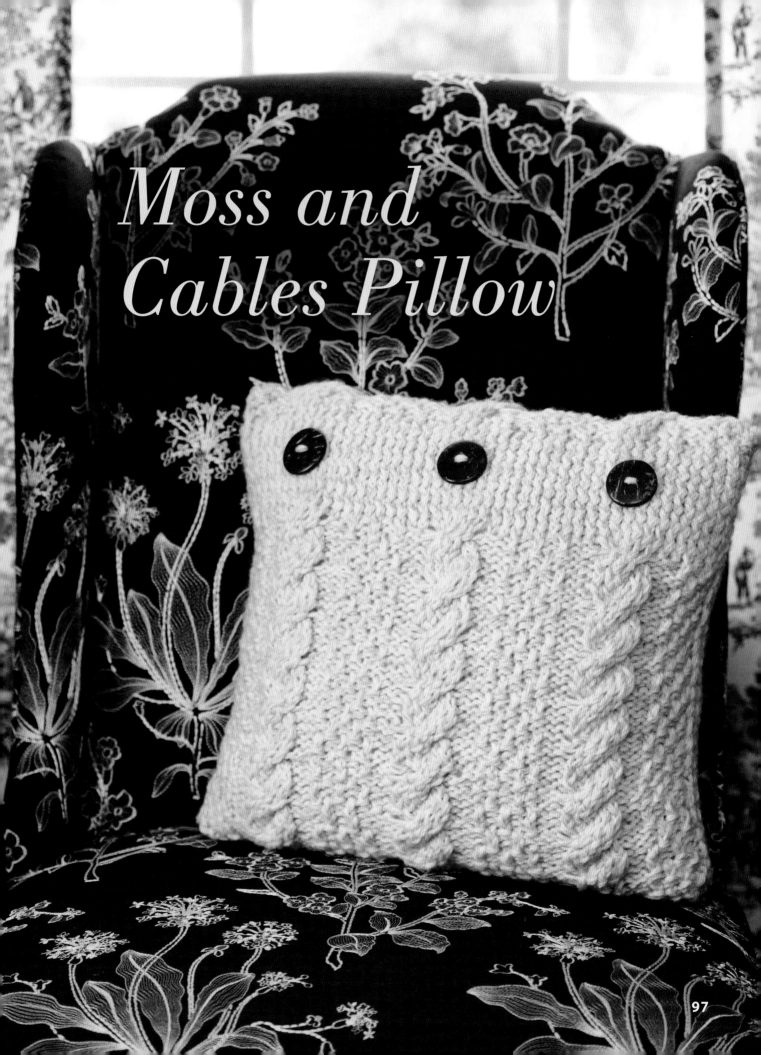

Moss and Cables Pillow

Three 6-stitch cables and panels of double moss stitch make this loom-knit pillow a classic home décor project! Full of texture and warmth, this pillow will fit into any style home. Finish it as a pillow or sew a zipper into the bottom seam and use it as a pillow cover.

Level

Intermediate to Advanced

Finished Measurements

16"/40.5 cm x 16"/40.5 cm

Gauge

10 sts and 16 rows in double moss stitch = 4"/10 cm square

Yarn

Plymouth Yarn Encore Chunky Colorspun, bulky weight #5 yarn (75% acrylic, 25% wool; 143 yd./131 m, 3.5 oz./100 g per skein)
2 skeins #7991 Drifting (MC)
Patons Classic Wool Worsted, medium worsted weight #4 yarn (100% wool; 210 yd./192 m, 3.5 oz./100 g per skein)
2 skeins #24407700201 Winter White (CC)

Supplies

- Round loom with 1/2"/1.25 cm peg spacing and at least 50 pegs
- 12 stitch markers
- Knitting tool
- Crochet hook
- Measuring tape
- 3 large buttons
- 16" x 16"/40.5 x 40.5 cm pillow form
- 16"/40.5 cm zipper (optional)

Pattern Notes

- Pattern is worked as a single flat panel, starting left to right, holding a strand each of the MC and CC and knitting them as one strand. The panel is then folded and seamed.
- Place stitch markers on pegs 6, 7, 14, 15, 21, 22, 29, 30, 36, 37, 44, and 45.

Pillow Cover

Using chain cast-on and holding 1 strand each MC and CC, cast on to 50 pegs; work as a flat panel.
Row 1: Ewk.
Rows 2 and 3: *Ewk1, p1, ewk1, p1, ewk1, p2, ewk6, p2, rep from * to end.
Rows 4 and 5: *P1, ewk1, p1, ewk1, p3, ewk6, p2, repeat from * to end.
Row 6: *Ewk1, p1, ewk1, p1, ewk1, p2, ewk6, p2, rep from * to end.
Row 7 (cable row): *Ewk1, p1, ewk1, p1, ewk1, p2, 6-st RC, p2, rep from * to end.
Rows 8 and 9: Repeat Rows 4 and 5.
Rows 10 and 11: Repeat Rows 2 and 3.
Row 12: *P1, ewk1, p1, ewk1, p3, ewk6, p2, rep from * to end.
Row 13 (cable row): *P1, ewk1, p1, ewk1, p3, 6-st RC, p2, rep from * to end.
Repeat Rows 2–13 until knitting measures 10"/20.5 cm in length, ending on cable row.
Ewk all rows until knitting measures 13 1/2"/34 cm in length, ending last row at starter peg.
Repeat Rows 2–13 until knitting measures 32 1/2"/82.5 cm if you would like the pillow cover to have a cabled back. If you prefer a plain back, continue to ewk all rows until knitting measures 32 1/2"/82.5 cm.
BO all sts using chain 1 bind-off.
Weave in ends.

Finishing

Fold the cover in half longways. Using mattress stitch and MC, seam the sides. If you want, sew a zipper along the bottom seam, then place the pillow form inside. Or, you can omit the zipper, place the form inside, and seam the bottom shut. Center one button on top border above each cable and sew on. Repeat for other two buttons.
Weave in ends.

Cable Shoulder Bag

One long cable frames the body of this purse and then continues up to form the strap. Another is used on the closure. Cables abound on this comfortable, everyday shoulder bag!

Level

Intermediate to Advanced

Finished Measurements

Body of bag: $10^1/_2$"/26.5 cm x 12"/30.5 cm
Strap: 33"/84 cm

Gauge

14 rows and 10 sts in stockinette stitch = 4"/10 cm square

Yarn

Patons Classic Wool Bulky, bulky weight #5 yarn (100% wool; 78 yd./71 m, 3.5 oz./100 g per skein)
3 skeins #24108989229 Natural Mix

Supplies

- 48-peg ($^5/_8$"/1.5 cm peg spacing) round loom
- 6 stitch markers
- Knitting tool
- Crochet hook
- Wood toggle or button
- Measuring tape
- Yarn or tapestry needle

Pattern Notes

- The bag is worked as separate flat panels, each starting left to right, and then sewn together.

Shoulder Bag

BORDER AND STRAP

Place stitch markers on pegs 3–8 to indicate where cable is to be worked. Using true cable cast-on, cast on to 10 pegs.
Rows 1–5: Ewk1, p1, ewk6, p1, k1.

Row 6 (cable row): K1, p1, 6-st RC, p1, k1.
Repeat Rows 1–6 until knitting measures 62"/157.5 cm.
BO all sts using chain 1 bind-off, leaving a 10"/25.5 cm tail.
Seam ends together using mattress stitch.

FRONT AND BACK PANELS (MAKE 2)

Using true cable cast-on, cast on to 26 pegs.
Row 1: Ewk.
Row 2: Knit.
Repeat Rows 1 and 2 until knitting measures $9^1/_2$"/24 cm.
Next row: Purl.
Next row: Ewk.
Repeat last two rows.
BO all sts using chain 1 bind-off.

CLOSURE STRAP

Place stitch markers on pegs 2–8 to indicate where cable is to be worked. Using true cable cast-on, cast on to 10 pegs.
Rows 1–4: Ewk1, p1, ewk6, p1, k1.
Row 5 (cable row): K1, p1, 6-st RC, p1, k1.
Repeat Rows 1–5 until knitting measures $6^1/_2$"/16.5 cm.
Next row: K1, k2tog, k4, ssk, k1.
Next row: P1, p2tog, p2, ssp, p1.
Next row: K2tog, k2, ssk.
Next row: P2tog, yo-p2tog
Next row: Knit.
BO all sts using chain 1 bind-off.
Weave in ends.

Assembly

With right sides facing out, align strap seam with bottom center of front panel; pin together and seam.
Align, pin, and seam together with the back panel.
Align center of closure with the top center of back panel; pin together and seam $^1/_2$"/1.25 cm down from top of bag opening. Fold over top of bag, align button or toggle, and sew to bag.
Weave in all ends.

Figure 8 Stitch and Puff Stitch

In addition to the stitch combinations you can make using knits and purls, you can also make stitches by doing different wraps on the pegs or by lifting stitches back up onto the loom. You'll learn two new stitches in this lesson: the figure 8 and the puff stitch. Both create a distinctive look in your knitted fabric.

Here is a sample of the figure 8 stitch done with a bulky yarn.

Here is a close-up of the fabric created by the puff stitch.

Figure 8 Stitch (FIG8 st)

This makes a big bold stitch with a loose weave.

1. Take the working yarn behind the two pegs you will work the stitch over (we'll call them pegs 1 and 2).

2. Wrap the yarn around to the front of peg 2, then thread it through pegs 1 and 2 to the center of the loom.

3. Wrap the yarn around to the front of peg 1, then between pegs 1 and 2 to the center of the loom.

4. Take bottom loop/stitch on peg 1 over the top stitch and top of the peg.

5. For the next stitch, you will take the working yarn behind pegs 2 and 3 and repeat Steps 2–4, this time knitting pegs 2 and 3, and then so on until all the pegs have been worked.

Note: If you are knitting in the round, your last stitch for the row/round will be on peg 1.
Note: You are working on pegs 1 and 2. Your next wrap would be on pegs 2 and 3 and so on. Essentially you will be double knitting each peg as you go around.

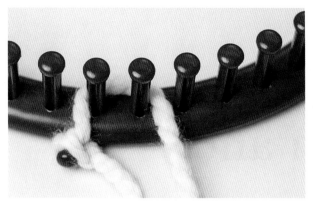

To illustrate this stitch more clearly, I am showing how the pegs are wrapped only. You, of course, would be doing this with stitches already on your loom. First, you take the working yarn behind the two pegs you will work the stitch over.

Bring the working yarn to the front of peg 2 and take the yarn between the two pegs, to the center of the loom.

Wrap the yarn around to the front of the first peg and then back through the two pegs to the center of the loom again (this is your figure 8).

Puff Stitch (PS)

Just as the name suggests, this stitch will add a puffy texture to your knitting. It is a good choice for items that require a lot of texture and warmth, like mitts and hats.

1. With the knitting tool, on the inside of the loom, reach down however many rows is indicated in the pattern (in this case, 5 rows) and pick the stitch up directly in line with that peg (be sure you've got the right stitch).

2. Place the stitch onto the peg.

3. Knit both stitches together as one.

4. Pull gently down on your knitting to loosen the stitch a bit.

Count down however many rows is indicated in the pattern and pick the stitch up directly under the peg you are working the puff stitch on.

Place the picked-up stitch onto the peg. Then knit both stitches (as one) over the working yarn and knob, completing the puff stitch.

Puff Stitch
Fingerless
Mitts

*Although they look complicated,
the e-wrap knit stitch makes fast work of these fingerless mitts.
Full of texture and style, these mitts are sure to please!*

Level

Confident Beginner

Finished Measurements

Approx. 8^1/$_2$"/21.5 cm long x 9^1/$_2$"/24 cm around (small/medium)

Gauge

12 sts and 24 rows in puff stitch and twisted stockinette (ewk) = 4"/10 cm square

Yarn

Premier Yarns Deborah Norville Serenity Baby, medium worsted weight #4 yarn (100% acrylic; 175 yd./160 m, 3.5 oz./100 g per skein)
1 skein #5002 Cream

Supplies

- 25-peg (^{1}/$_2$"/1.25 cm peg spacing) round loom
- Knitting tool
- Crochet hook
- 4 buttons
- Needle and embroidery thread (for buttons)

Pattern Notes

- Pattern is worked in the round, then back and forth in rows to create the thumb opening, then in the round to finish.

Mitts (make 2)

Using chain cast-on, cast on to all pegs; join to work in the round.

Rnds 1–16: *P2, k2, rep from * to last peg, ewk1.
Rnds 17–21: Ewk.
Rnd 22: *PS1, ewk3, rep from * until last peg, ewk1.
Rnds 23–40: Repeat Rnds 17–22 three times.

THUMB

Stop working in the round; work as a flat panel, changing directions at the end of each row to create the thumb opening.

Rows 1–5: Ewk.
Row 6: *PS1, ewk3, rep from * until last peg, ewk1.

TOP OF MITT

Begin working in the round again.
Rnds 1–5: Ewk.
Rnd 6: *PS1, ewk3, rep from * until last peg, ewk1.
Rnds 7 and 9: Purl.
Rnds 8 and 10: Knit.
BO all sts using chain 1 bind-off (for small hands) or extra stretchy bind-off (for larger hands).

Finishing

Weave in ends.
Sew two buttons on the outside cuff of each mitt.

The Little Bear Hooded Cowl

Both adorable and practical, this quick loom-knit project will fit children of any size!

Level

Confident Beginner

Finished Measurements

22"/56 cm around neck and 13"/33 cm high

Gauge

8 sts and 9 rows in figure 8 stitch = 4"/10 cm square

Yarn

Lion Brand Wool-Ease Thick and Quick, super bulky weight #6 yarn (82% acrylic, 10% wool, 8% rayon; 106 yd./97 m, 5 oz./140 g per skein)
2 skeins #640-124 Barley

Supplies

- 41-peg ($^3/_4$"/2 cm peg spacing) round loom
- 12-peg ($^3/_4$"/2 cm peg spacing) flower, round loom
- Knitting tool
- Crochet hook
- Yarn or tapestry needle
- Large button
- Small pom-pom maker (or make your own)

Pattern Notes

- Pattern is worked counterclockwise in the round to create the neck, then back and forth in a flat panel for the hood, which is then seamed at the top. The ears are knit separately, then sewn on.

Cowl

Using 41-peg loom and chain cast-on, cast on to all pegs; join to work in the round.
Rnd 1: Ewk.
Rnd 2: Purl.
Rnds 3–12: FIG8 st around.
BO 10 pegs with chain 1 bind-off.

HOOD

Stop working in the round; work as a flat panel over remaining pegs.
Rows 1–15: FIG8 st.
BO all sts using chain 1 bind-off.
Fasten off, leaving a tail long enough to seam top of hood.

Finishing

Align the corners and fold the hood in half with RS facing out. Seam from front to back.
Weave in ends.
Sew on button.
Make two small pom-poms (see page 12); tie pom-poms together with a 10"/25.5 cm piece of yarn; secure to button.

BEAR EARS (MAKE 2)

Using 12-peg loom and e-wrap cast-on, cast on to all pegs, join to work in the round.
Rows 1–7: Ewk.
BO all sts using gather method, leaving tail long enough to seam ear closed and sew on to hood.
Gather ear halfway closed, then turn inside out and seam closed, keeping ear rounded.
With RS out, flatten ear and thread a gather stitch (go in and out of each stitch at the bottom of ear) all the way around the ear $^1/_4$"/.5 cm in from the edges; use this stitch to slightly gather the ear until it starts to bend. Sew onto the top of the hood $1^3/_4$"/4.5 cm from the front edge.
Repeat for the other ear.

Newborn Football Baby Cocoon

Loom knit this cozy newborn cocoon, with its handmade football buttons, in one weekend! And don't forget the matching hat (page 110)!

Level

Confident Beginner

Finished Measurements

20"/51 cm long x 18"/46 cm around

Gauge

10 sts and 14 rows in pattern stitch = 4"/10 cm square

Yarn

Caron Simply Soft, medium worsted weight #4 yarn (100% acrylic; 315 yd./288 m, 6 oz./170 g per skein
  2 skeins #H970039750 Chocolate
Lion Brand Pound of Love, medium worsted weight #4 yarn (100% acrylic; 1,020 yd./932 m, 16 oz./454 g per skein)
  1 skein #550-100 White (CC)

Supplies

- 41-peg (³/₄"/2 cm peg spacing) round loom
- Knitting tool
- Crochet hook
- Yarn needle
- Small or medium pom-pom maker (or make your own)
- 2 store-bought buttons, if not making your own

Pattern Notes

- Cocoon is worked on all the pegs as a flat panel, starting left to right, for 15 rows, then joined to work in the round.
- Work two strands of the MC and the CC as one; since the Pound of Love is such a big skein, wind it into two balls.

Cocoon

Using two strands MC and chain cast-on, cast on to all pegs. *Do not* join to work in the round.

Rows 1, 3, and 5: U-knit.
Rows 2 and 4: Purl.
Row 6: Ewk.
Row 7: K2, yo-k2tog, k33, yo-k2tog, k2.
Even-numbered rows 8–14: Ewk.
Odd-numbered rows 9–15: U-knit.
Row 16: Ewk; at the end of this row, join to work in the round.
Rnds 17, 19, and 21: U-knit.
Rnds 18, 20, and 22: Ewk.
Drop MC. Pick up two strands CC and work as one.
Rnd 23: U-knit.
Rnd 24: Ewk.
Rnd 25: U-knit.
Cut CC. Pick up two strands MC and work as one.
Rnd 26: Ewk.
Rnd 27: U-knit.
Repeat [Rnds 26 and 27] 16 times.
Drop MC. Pick up two strands of CC.
Next rnd: Ewk.
Next rnd: U-knit.
Next rnd: Ewk.
Cut CC. Pick up two strands MC.
Next rnd: U-knit.
Next rnd: Ewk.
Repeat last two rnds six times.
BO all sts using gather method.

Finishing

Turn cocoon inside out. Shape the bottom by seaming it closed completely using mattress stitch.

Fold over the collar of cocoon, then line up and sew on buttons or make your own (see below).

Using the chart, add laces to your cocoon by weaving in and out of your knitting with needle and yarn. Center your design on the front of your knitting between the two white stripe sections.

Make two small pom-poms (see page 12) using either the MC or CC or both, and then attach to the top middle of the cocoon.

I-CORD FOOTBALL BUTTONS

Using two strands MC and chain cast-on, cast on to 3 pegs on large-gauge loom.

Rows 1–5: Knit peg 1, knit peg 3, then knit peg 2.

BO all sts using chain 1 bind-off and pull tight. Cut working yarn, leaving 17"/43 cm tail.

Thread yarn tail onto yarn needle and blanket stitch around football button. Weave in ends, leaving 6"/15 cm tail for sewing onto garment.

Use one strand of CC to sew laces onto button.

Football Lace Chart for Cocoon

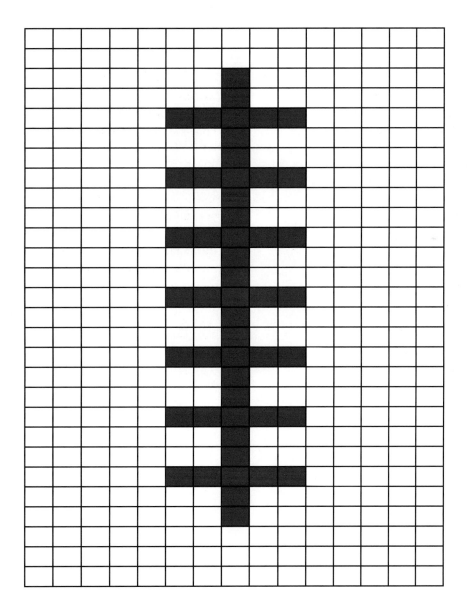

Infant
Football
Hat

This is adorable worked in the newborn size to match the cocoon, but it's so cute you'll want the larger size as well. It's amazing how fast babies' heads grow!

Level

Beginner

Sizes

Newborn (3–12 months)

Finished Measurements

9.6"/24 cm (14.4"/36.5 cm) circumference, 6"/15.25 cm (7.25"/18.5 cm) length

Gauge

10 sts and 16 rows in pattern stitch = 4"/10 cm square

Yarn

Caron Simply Soft, medium worsted weight #4 yarn (100% acrylic; 315 yd./288 m, 6 oz./170 g per skein) 2 skeins #H970039750 Chocolate

Lion Brand Pound of Love, medium worsted weight #4 yarn (100% acrylic; 1,020 yd./932 m, 16 oz./454 g per skein) 1 skein #550-100 White (CC) (you will only need 50 yd./48 m)

Supplies

- 24-peg (³/₄"/2 cm peg spacing) round loom for newborn size or 36-peg (¹¹/₁₆"/1.75 cm peg spacing) round loom for 3–12 months size
- Knitting tool
- Crochet hook
- Small or medium pom-pom maker (or make your own)

Pattern Notes

- The hat is worked in the round counterclockwise, holding two strands of yarn and working them together as one.
- For longer-lasting fit, it is recommended that you make the larger 3–12 months size hat.

Newborn Size Only

Using two strands MC and chain cast-on, cast on to all pegs counterclockwise; join to work in the round.

Rnd 1: Ewk.
Rnd 2: U-knit.
Rnd 3: Ewk.
Drop MC. Pick up two strands of CC.
Rnd 4: U-knit.
Rnd 5: Ewk.
Cut CC. Pick up MC.
Even-numbered rnds 6–14: U-knit.
Odd-numbered rnds 7–13: Ewk.
Drop MC. Pick up two strands CC.
Rnd 15: Ewk.
Rnd 16: U-knit.
Cut CC. Pick up two strands MC.
Odd-numbered rnds 17–23: Ewk.
Even-numbered rnds 18–24: U-knit.
BO all sts using gather method.
Weave in all ends.

3–12 Months Only

Rnds 1 and 3: Ewk.

Rnds 2 and 4: U-knit.

Drop MC. Pick up two strands of CC.

Rnd 5: Ewk.

Rnd 6: U-knit.

Cut CC. Pick up MC.

Odd-numbered rnds 7–19: Ewk.

Even-numbered rnds 8–18: Knit.

Drop MC. Pick up two strands CC.

Rnd 20: U-knit.

Rnd 21: Ewk.

Cut CC. Pick up two strands MC.

Even-numbered rnds 22–28: U-knit.

Odd-numbered rnds 23–29: Ewk.

BO all sts using gather method.

Weave in all ends.

Finishing for Both Sizes

Using chart, with white yarn and yarn needle, stitch football laces on center front of hat by going in and out of knitting.

Make a small or medium pom-pom (see page 12) using equal amounts of MC and CC or one color only. Secure to hat.

Football Lace Chart for Hat

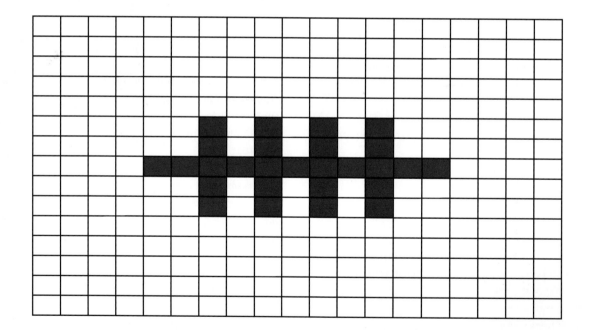

Fair Isle Cowl and Mitten Set

Add a touch of spring color to your wardrobe this winter!
This project is perfect for the first time Fair Isle knitter.

Level

Confident Beginner

Finished Measurements

Cowl: 8"/20.5 cm high (crown to brim), 28"/71 cm
   circumference
Mittens: 10"/25.5 cm circumference, length will vary

Gauge

Cowl: 6 sts and 18 rows in stockinette stitch = 4"/10 cm
   square
Mittens: 15 sts and 18 rows in stockinette stitch = 4"/10 cm
   square

Yarn

Patons Classic Wool Bulky, bulky weight #5 yarn
   (100% wool; 78 yd./71 m, 3.5 oz./100 g per skein)

Cowl

   2 skeins #24108989223 Spring Green (MC)
   1 skein #24108989008 Aran (CC)

Mittens

   1 skein #24108989223 Spring Green (MC)
   1 skein #24108989008 Aran (CC)

Supplies

- 108-peg ($^3/_8$"/1 cm peg spacing) round loom (for cowl)
- 25-peg ($^1/_2$"/1.25 cm peg spacing) or 27-peg (for
   medium/large size) round loom (for mittens)
- Knitting tool
- Small crochet hook
- Measuring tape

Pattern Notes

- Cowl is worked in the round.
- The mitten pattern is sized for small ladies/teen. For a
   medium/large size, work the pattern on a 27-peg loom.
- The mittens are worked on all pegs in the round to the
   base of the thumb. At that point, you switch to back-
   and-forth knitting over just 6 pegs for the specified
   number of rows. You can add rows if your measurements differ from those of the pattern. The thumb folds
   back on itself (lengthwise) and will be seamed at the
   sides and top when finished. When the thumb flap is
   complete, you will go back to knitting in the round on
   all pegs to complete the top of the mitten, which will be
   seamed at the top when you are finished.

Cowl

Using 108-peg loom, MC, and chain cast-on, cast on to all
   pegs; join to work in the round.
Rnds 1 and 3: Knit.
Rnds 2 and 4: Purl.
Begin Fair Isle pattern; add CC.
Rnd 5: *K1 with MC, k1 with CC, rep from * to end.
Rnd 6: *K1 with CC, k1 with MC, rep from * to end.
Repeat Rnds 5 and 6 until knitting measures $7^1/_2$"/19 cm.
Cut CC.
Using MC, repeat Rnds 1–4.
BO all sts using chain 1 bind-off.
Weave in ends.
Block knitting.

Fair Isle Mittens (make 2)

Using 25- or 27-peg loom, MC, and chain cast-on, cast on
to all pegs; join to work in the round.
Rnds 1–18: *K2, p2, rep from * to last peg, k1.
Begin Fair Isle pattern; add CC.
Rnd 19: *K1 with MC, k1 with CC, rep from * to end.
Rnd 20: *K1 with CC, k1 with MC, rep from * to end.
Rnds 21–26: Repeat Rnds 19 and 20 three times.
For perfect fit, measure the distance between your wrist
and thumb, then add rows here if needed.

THUMB

Knit short rows over 6 pegs only.
Rows 1–20: *K1 with MC, k1 with CC, rep from *.
For perfect fit, measure length of your thumb, then add
more rows here if needed.

TOP OF MITTEN

Start knitting in the round again.
Rnd 1: *K1 with MC, k1 with CC, rep from * to end.
Rnd 2: *K1 with CC, k1 with MC, rep from * to end.
Rnds 3–20: Repeat Rnds 1 and 2 nine times.
Cut CC. Use MC only.
Rnds 21–24: Knit.
Place your hand through the loom and check the length of
the mitten. Just your fingertips should be sticking out of
the top of the knitting. Add rows here if needed.
BO alls sts using gather method, leaving a long tail for
seaming.

Finishing

With right side facing out, pull gently on yarn to gather
just the edges of the top of each mitten (to round), then
seam the top closed using mattress stitch.
Fold thumb in half lengthwise with right side facing out
and seam top and side of thumb closed using mattress
stitch.

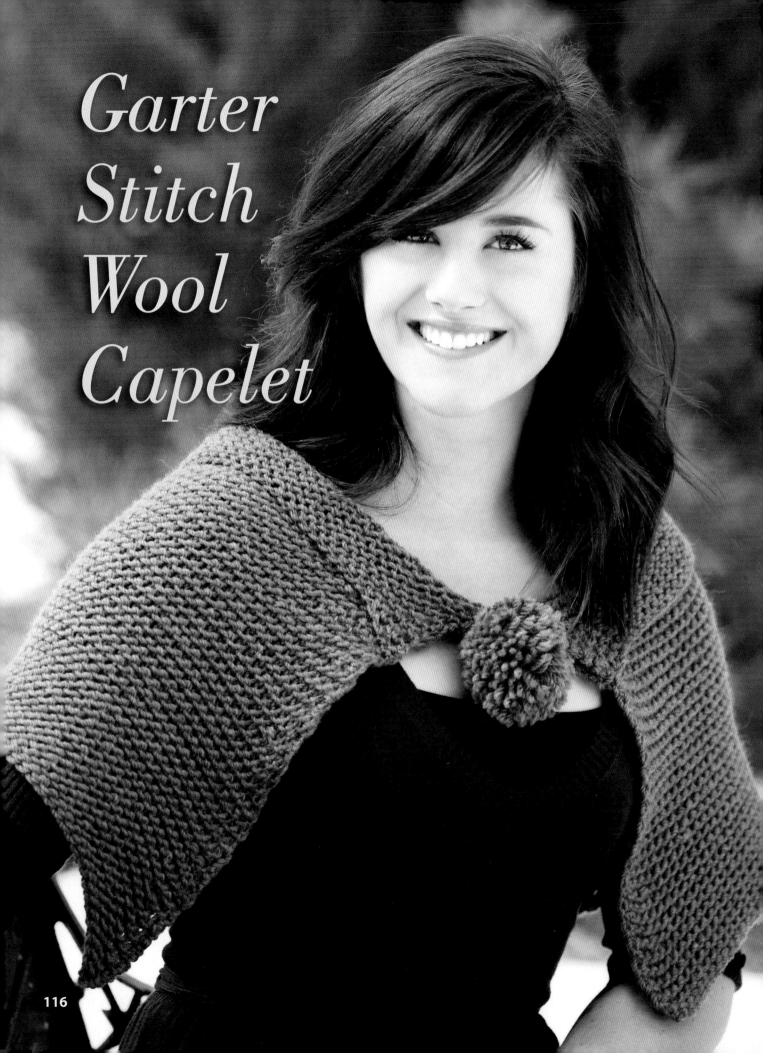

Garter Stitch Wool Capelet

This elegant capelet features a pom-pom and I-cord closure.

Level

Intermediate+

Sizes

Small/Medium (Large/XL)

Finished Measurements

Length at lower edge: 46$\frac{1}{2}$"/118 cm (48"/123 cm)
Width: 10"/25.5 cm (all sizes)

Gauge

12 sts and 14 rows in garter stitch = 4"/10 cm square

Yarn

Patons Classic Wool Worsted, medium worsted weight #4
    yarn (100% wool; 210 yd./192 m, 3.5 oz./100 g per skein)
    1 skein #24407777115 New Denim

Supplies

* 66-peg ($\frac{1}{2}$"/1.25 cm peg spacing) round loom
* Knitting tool
* Crochet hook
* Measuring tape
* Tapestry or yarn needle
* Large pom-pom maker (or make your own)

Pattern Notes

* Capelet is constructed from two panels that are seamed together.
* The panels are gently decreased to create a soft curve around the shoulders and neck.

Capelet Panel (make 2)

Using chain cast-on, cast on to 64 (66) pegs; do not join to
    work in the round.
Rows 1 and 3: Sk1, ewk to end.
Rows 2 and 4: Sk1, p to end.
Rows 5–12: Repeat Rows 1–4 two times.
Row 13: Sk1, ewk2, k2tog, ewk56 (58), ssk, ewk2.
Rows 14 and 16: Sk1, p to end.
Row 15: Sk1, ewk to end.
Rows 17–20: Repeat Rows 15 and 16 two times.
Row 21: Sk1, ewk2, k2tog, ewk54 (56), ssk, ewk2.
Row 22: Sk1, p to end.
Row 23: Sk1, ewk to end.
Rows 24–29: Repeat Rows 22 and 23 three times.
Row 30: Sk1, p to end.
Row 31: Sk1, ewk2, k2tog, ewk52 (54), ssk, ewk2.
Rows 32–37: Repeat Rows 22 and 23 three times.
Row 38: Sk1, p to end.
Row 39: Sk1, ewk2, k2tog, ewk50 (52), ssk, ewk2.
Rows 40–57: Repeat Rows 22 and 23 nine times.
Row 58: Sk1, p to end.
Row 59: Sk1, ewk2, k2tog, ewk48 (50), ssk, ewk2.
Rows 60–77: Repeat Rows 22 and 23 nine times.
Row 78: Sk1, p to end.
Row 79: Sk1, ewk2, k2tog, ewk46 (48), ssk, ewk2.
Rows 80–89: Repeat Rows 22 and 23 five times.
BO all sts using chain 1 bind-off.

Finishing

Weave in ends.

Block knitting.

Once the pieces are totally dry, line the edges up as shown in the diagram.

Using the garter seam (see page 10), seam the panels together on the right side of the knitting starting at the bottom and stopping 3"/7.5 cm from the top.

Fold the collar down 3"/7.5 cm.

Continue seaming the pieces together on right side of knitting.

Also, if you like, you can hold the collar in place with stitches at the front folds and back seam if desired.

Make a 3^1/$_2$"/8 cm to 4"/10 cm pom-pom (page 12) and sew it to the left top of capelet.

Make a 3^1/$_2$"/8 cm long I-cord (page 51) and sew one end to the right, top side of capelet and the other end 1^1/$_4$"/3 cm below, forming a loop.

To close capelet, lift the loop over the pom-pom.

Diagram for Seaming the Panels Together

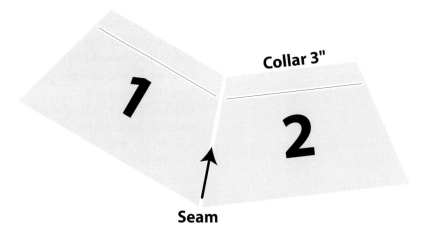

Classic Christmas Stocking

Add a family treasure to your mantel this year by loom knitting this classic wool stocking! Intarsia is used to loom knit the trees in this project.

Level

Intermediate

Finished Measurements

26"/66 cm long x 5"/12.5 cm wide; 11"/28 cm around

Gauge

16 sts and 24 rows in stockinette stitch = 4"/10 cm square

Yarn

Brown Sheep Company Lamb's Pride Bulky, bulky weight
 #5 yarn (85% wool, 15% mohair; 125 yd./114 m,
 3.5 oz./100 g per skein)
 1 skein #M10 Crème
 1 skein #M197 Red Hot Passion

Supplies

- 36-peg (1/2"/1.25 cm peg spacing) round loom
- Stitch markers
- Knitting tool
- Crochet hook
- Tapestry or yarn needle

Pattern Notes

- Pattern is worked counterclockwise in the round.
- Before starting, place a stitch marker on peg 18. This will mark the center of the Christmas tree and where you will start the intarsia pattern. The chart is worked from left to right, from the top down.
- When knitting the trees, do not carry the CC, drop it after the last CC st is knit. Twist MC and CC together whenever they meet.
- Pay careful attention to color changes throughout pattern.

Christmas Stocking

Using CC and chain cast-on, cast on to all pegs; join to work in the round.

Rnds 1–10: *K2, p2, rep from *.

Rnd 11: Knit.

Drop CC and pick up MC.

Rnds 12–16: Knit.

Drop MC and pick up CC.

Rnds 17–19: Knit.

Drop CC and pick up MC.

Rnds 20–22: Knit.

Rnds 23–42: Knit with CC and MC, following chart for 20 rows.

Drop CC.

Rnds 43–45: Knit.

Drop MC and pick up CC.

Rnds 46–48: Knit.

Drop CC and pick up MC.

Rnds 49–51: Knit.

Rows 52–71: Knit with CC and MC, following the chart.

Drop CC.

Rnds 72–74: Knit.

Drop MC and pick up CC.

Rnds 75–77: Knit.

Drop CC and pick up MC.

Rnds 78–80: Knit.

Drop MC and pick up CC.

Rnds 81–83: Knit.

Drop CC and pick up MC.

Rnds 84–93: Knit.

Drop MC and pick up CC.

Rnds 94–96: Knit.

Drop CC and pick up MC.

Rnds 97–99: Knit.

Drop MC and pick up CC.

Rnds 100–102: Knit.

Drop CC and pick up MC.

Rnds 103–112: Knit.

BEGIN HEEL

Using CC only, heel will be worked in short rows with wrap & turn over 18 pegs.

Row 1: Starting on peg 10, k9, w&t peg 19.

Row 2: K18, w&t peg 36.

Row 3: K17, w&t peg 18.

Row 4: K16, w&t peg 1.

Rows 5–13: Continue knitting across, then w&t the peg before last wrapped peg (decreasing).

Rows 14–22: Knit across to the first wrapped peg, knit wrapped peg, w&t the next peg (increasing).

Row 23: K9.

Heel is finished.

FOOT

Begin knitting in the round.

Drop CC and pick up MC.

Rnds 24–33: Knit.

Drop MC and pick up CC.

Rnds 34–36: Knit.

Drop CC and pick up MC.

Rnds 37–39: Knit.

Drop MC and pick up CC.

Rnds 40–42: Knit.

Drop CC and pick up MC.

Rnds 43–52: Knit.

Drop MC and pick up CC.

Rnds 53–62: Knit.

BO all sts using gather method.

Weave in ends.

Hanger

Make a 4"/10 cm long I-cord (page 51) or braid three strands CC; attach both ends to top of stocking to create hanger loop.

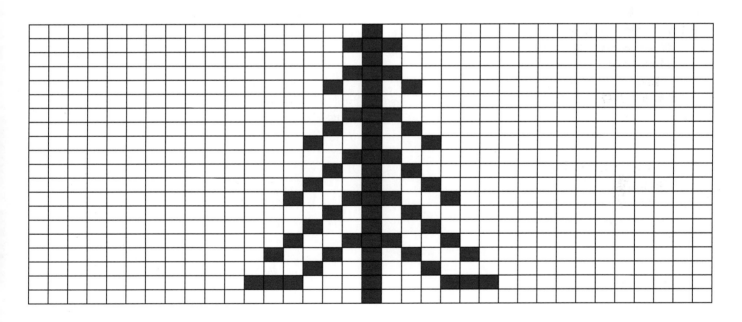

Chart works from the top down and starts on peg 1, working left to right.

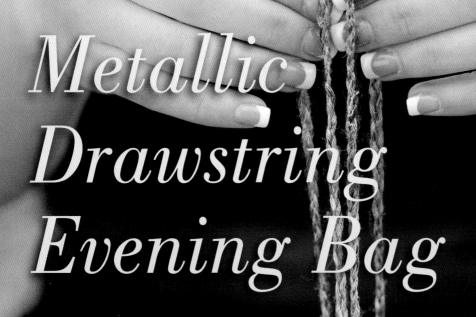

Metallic Drawstring Evening Bag

*Lace and ridge stitches give this lovely little purse
plenty of texture and the metallic yarn a stylish, contemporary look.
It's the perfect size for a night on the town!*

Level

Intermediate

Finished Measurements

7"/18 cm x 8"/20 cm; bag opens a full 8"/20 cm.

Gauge

Not essential to this pattern

Yarn

Patons Metallic, medium worsted weight #4 yarn
(63% nylon, 28% acrylic, 9% wool; 252 yd./230 m,
3 oz./85 g per skein)
1 skein #24409595044 Pewter

Supplies

- 66-peg ($^1/_2$"/1.25 cm peg spacing) round loom
- Knitting tool
- Crochet hook
- Tapestry or yarn needle
- 15"/38 cm x 15"/38 cm square of satin fabric
- Sewing needle and thread to match satin fabric

Pattern Notes

- Pattern is worked counterclockwise in the round.

Purse

Using e-wrap cast-on, cast on to all pegs.
Rnd 1: Ewk.
Rnd 2: Purl.
Rnd 3: Ewk.
Rnd 4: Ew-ssk around.
Rnd 5: Ewk.
Rnd 6: Purl.
Rnd 7: Ewk.

Rnd 8: Ew-k2tog around.
Rnds 9–32: Repeat Rnds 1–8 three times.
Rnd 33: Ewk.
Rnd 34: Purl.
Rnd 35: Ewk.
BO all sts using chain 1 bind-off.
Weave in ends.

DRAWSTRINGS (MAKE 2)

Cut three pieces of yarn 25"/63.5 cm or longer; knot to-
gether, leaving 2"/5 cm of tassel.
Braid strands together.
Knot end, leaving 2"/5 cm tassel.
Repeat for second drawstring.

Finishing

Measure down approximately 2"/5 cm below top of bag
and weave tassel of one drawstring in and out halfway
around the opening of bag. Tie the ends of the drawstring together and leave hang in the center of bag.
Repeat with the second drawstring around the other
half of the opening.

Push tassels from one drawstring through the front of the
purse. Skip a lace opening and push the tassels from the
other drawstring through that hole. Using a yarn needle,
sew all tassels together through the knots, then sew to
the front of your bag (this will prevent them from being
pulled into the inside of the bag when opening it. You
can now grab the center drawstrings to use as handles
and gather the bag.

Line the bag with satin fabric before using; attach liner
below drawstrings (see page 77 for a tutorial).

Rainbow Baby Bib

*So sweet and colorful,
this bib will fit babies up to three years.*

Level

Beginner

Finished Measurements

10"/25 cm square, strap 9"/23 cm long

Gauge

12 sts and 14 rows in pattern stitch = 4"/10 cm square

Yarn

Lion Brand Baby Soft, light worsted weight #3 yarn
(60% acrylic, 40% polyamide; 459 yd./420 m, 5 oz./
141 g per skein)
1 skein #920-143 Lavender (MC)
1 skein #920-157 Pastel Yellow (CC1)
1 skein #920-101 Pastel Pink (CC2)
1 skein #920-106 Pastel Blue (CC3)
1 skein #920-100 Crisp White (CC4; optional)

Supplies

- 31-peg ($^3/_4$"/2 cm peg spacing) round loom
  (23 pegs used)
- Knitting tool
- Crochet hook
- Medium button
- Yarn needle

Pattern Notes

- The bib is worked as a flat panel, starting left to right,
  holding two strands of yarn and working them as one
  throughout.
- The strap is worked directly from the bib by doing a
  partial bind-off and continuing to work the strap; read
  The Partial Bind-Off or Cast-On (page 50) before starting
  this project.

Bib

Using two strands MC and true cable cast-on, cast on to
23 pegs of the loom.
Rows 1 and 2: Ewk.
Row 3: Purl.
Rows 4 and 5: Ewk.
Row 6: Purl.
Row 7: Ewk.
Cut MC, pick up CC1.
Row 8: Ewk.
Row 9: Purl.
Rows 10 and 11: Ewk.
Row 12: Purl.
Row 13: Ewk.
Cut CC1, pick up CC2.
Rows 14–19: Repeat Rows 8–13.
Cut CC2, pick up CC3.
Rows 20–25: Repeat Rows 8–13.
Cut CC3, pick up CC2.
Rows 26–31: Repeat Rows 8–13.
Row 32: Ewk.
Row 33: BO 18 sts using the chain 1 bind-off, p5.

STRAP

You will now be working in short rows over 5 pegs.
Rows 34 and 35: Ewk.
Row 36: Purl.
Rows 37–75: Repeat [Rows 34–36] 13 times.
BO remaining 5 sts using chain 1 bind-off.

Finishing

Weave in all ends.
Sew button on top left corner of bib. You can push the
button through the knitting; no button hole is needed.
For added decoration, you can blanket stitch around the
outside of the bib with CC4, if you like.

Mesh
Triangle
Scarf

You can make this beautiful accent piece with just one ball of yarn. Use metallic yarn for a dressy feel or acrylic for a more casual look.

Level

Confident beginner

Finished Measurements

44"/112 cm on longest edge, 16"/41.5 cm deep

Gauge

8 sts and 8 rows in chainmail stitch = 4"/10 cm square

Yarn

Patons Metallic, medium worsted weight #4 yarn
(63% nylon, 28% acrylic, 9% wool; 252 yd./230 m,
3 oz./85 g per skein)
1 skein #24409595219 Metallic Sea Breeze

Supplies

- 48-peg ($^5/_8$"/1.5 cm peg spacing) round loom
- Knitting tool
- Crochet hook
- Yarn needle

Pattern Notes

- Pattern is worked as a flat panel, starting left to right.
- The lovely open chainmail effect is created by skipping every other peg as you work across the rows.
- The triangle shape of this scarf is created by knitting sideways and gradually increasing, then decreasing, the number of stitches.

Scarf

Place a slipknot on peg 1.
Row 1: Ewk.
Row 2: Ewk1, skip next peg, e-wrap next empty peg.
Row 3: Ewk.
Row 4: *Ewk1, sk1, repeat from * to last stitch, e-wrap first empty peg.

Repeat Rows 3 and 4 until all pegs on loom have loops on them.
Next row: Ewk.
Next row: Ew-k2tog, *sk1, ewk1, rep from * to end of row.
Next row: Ewk.
Repeat the last two rows until there is only one peg with a stitch on it.
Bind off.

Finishing

Weave in ends.
Add 4"/10 cm fringe to three sides of your triangle (see page 15).

Lady's
Knit
Shrug

This lovely little cover-up is just the answer when the evening turns just a bit chilly. With gentle shaping through the arms and around the collar, this shrug provides a comfortable fit and maximum style.

Level

Confident Beginner

Sizes

Small/Medium (Large)

Finished Measurements

Garment will vary in width, depending on the loom; 22"/56 cm long

Gauge

12 sts and 18 rows in garter stitch = 4"/10 cm square

Yarn

Lion Brand Vanna's Choice, medium worsted weight #4 yarn (100% acrylic; 145 yd./133 m, 3 oz./85 g per skein) 4 skeins #860-405 Silver Heather

Supplies

- 41-peg (³/4"/2 cm peg spacing) round loom
- Knitting tool
- Crochet hook
- Yarn or tapestry needle
- Measuring tape

Pattern Notes

- Pattern is worked knitting two strands of yarn as one.
- Garment is knit sideways in garter stitch.
- To make border/collar on this garment, you will place one side of the shrug back on the loom. To do this, you'll place one stitch on each peg from the first row of stitches.

Shrug

FIRST SLEEVE

Using two strands and chain cast-on, cast on to pegs 9–32 (8–33).

Row 1: *K2, p2, rep from * to end.

Row 2: *P2, k2, rep from * to end.

Rows 3–10: Repeat Rows 1 and 2 four times.

Rows 11–13: Knit to end, then e-wrap next 2 empty pegs. Second wrapped peg is first peg to be worked on next row.

Rows 14–16: Purl to end, then e-wrap next 2 empty pegs. Second wrapped peg is first peg to be worked on next row.

Repeat Rows 11–16 until all the pegs have stitches on them. First sleeve is now complete.

SHOULDER/BACK

Measure from the center of your upper arm (between the shoulder and elbow) to the opposite shoulder.

Continue knitting as flat panel, alternating 3 knit rows and 3 purl rows until this portion equals this measurement.

SECOND SLEEVE

Rows 1–3: K1, k2tog, knit to last 3 pegs, ssk, k1.

Rows 4–6: P1, p2tog, purl to last 3 pegs, ssp, p1.

Repeat Rows 1–6 until you have stitches on 24 (26) pegs.

Second Cuff

Row 1: *K2, p2, rep from * to end.

Row 2: *P2, k2, repeat from * to end.

Rows 3–10: Repeat Rows 1 and 2 four times.

BO all sts with chain 1 bind-off.

Finishing

Weave in ends.

Fold knitting in half and seam from start of cuff to where knitting stops increasing (about 9"/23 cm); repeat for other arm.

ADD COLLAR AND BORDER

From underarm seam to underarm seam, place one side of shrug back on the loom. Place one stitch on each peg (from first row of stitches).

Rows 1–3: Knit.

Row 4: P1, p2tog, purl all until last 3 pegs, ssp, p1.

Row 5: Purl.

Row 6: Repeat Row 4.

Row 7: K1, k2tog, knit all to last 3 pegs, ssk, k1.

Row 8: Knit.

Row 9: Repeat Row 7.

Row 10: Purl.

Row 11: Repeat Row 4.

Row 12: Purl.

Row 13: Repeat Row 7.

Row 14: Knit.

BO all sts using chain 1 bind-off.

Weave in ends.

Repeat above for second side of shrug.

Guide to Popular Round Looms

Brand	In Production	Adjustable	Available Numbers of Pegs	Gauge	Available Peg Spacing
Boye	Yes	No	24–40	Large	$5/8"$–$13/16"$
Loops-n-Threads	Yes	No	24–41	Large	$3/8"$–$13/16"$
Stitch Studio by Nicole	Yes	No	24–40	Large	$5/8"$–$13/16"$
CinDWood	Yes	No	10–146	Fine to large	$3/8"$–$3/4"$
Knifty Knitter	No, but widely available online	No	12–48	Large	$5/8"$–$13/16"$
Knitting Board	Yes	Yes	16–106	Fine to large	$3/16"$–$3/4"$
Cottage Looms	Yes	No, but can be customized	24–100s	Fine to large	$3/16"$–$3/4"$
Martha Stewart	Yes	Yes	300 Piece Kit	Small to large	$3/8"$–$3/4"$

Note: This is not an exhaustive list of available round looms. Long looms that allow knitting in the round have also been included in this list.

Loom Comparison by Peg Spacing and Number of Pegs

Peg Spacing							
$3/4"$	1	2	3	4	5	6	7
$5/8"$	$1^1/5$	$2^2/5$	$3^3/5$	$4^4/5$	6	$7^1/5$	$8^2/5$
$1/2"$	$1^1/2$	3	$4^1/2$	6	$7^1/2$	9	$10^1/2$
$7/16"$	$1^5/7$	$3^3/7$	$5^1/7$	$6^6/7$	$8^4/7$	$10^2/7$	12
$3/8"$	2	4	6	8	10	12	14
$1/4"$	3	6	9	12	15	18	21
Inches							
$3/4"$	$1^1/2"$	$2^1/4"$	$3"$	$3^3/4"$	$4^1/2"$	$5^1/4"$	

Note: This chart is for general comparison and is meant to be a guideline only. It assumes all pegs are set perfectly and it is a mathematical comparison of the number of pegs in a given number of inches for a particular peg spacing. Use it as a starting point when converting a pattern so you can use it with a loom with a peg spacing different than the one called for; I've given you two examples below of how to do this. The chart does not take into consideration shrinkage or different yarns and stitches.

Example 1: Your pattern calls for a loom with $3/4"$ peg spacing and you want to use a loom with $3/8"$ peg spacing.

Every 1 peg on the $3/4"$ loom is equal to 2 pegs on the $3/8"$ loom. So if the pattern calls for you to cast on 14 stitches, you will need to cast 28 stitches on the smaller gauge loom.

Example 2: Your pattern calls for a loom with $5/8"$ peg spacing and you want to use a loom with $3/4"$ peg spacing. To get to an even number of pegs, your stitch count will need to be a multiple of 5 pegs. If this is not possible, then you will have to either add or subtract pegs and settle for a close number of stitches. Loom knit a swatch and check for gauge before starting.

QUICK STITCH GUIDE

Note: When changing direction, you will get the mirror image of each of these sts. This has been accounted for in each pattern.

d-ewk E-wrap the peg, pull the bottom loop over the top loop (ewk). Repeat, then move to the next peg.

ewk Working back to front, wind the working yarn around the peg. Pull the bottom loop over the top loop.

ew-k2tog/p2tog
Move loop from peg 1 to peg 2, e-wrap peg 1, knit or purl the loops on peg 2 as one over working yarn.

ew-ssk/ew-ssp
Move loops from peg 2 to peg 1, knit or purl the loops on peg 1 as one over working yarn, next e-wrap peg 2.

fl-k Push the existing loops on each peg down to the bottom of loom. Position the working yarn above the loop on the peg, and pull the bottom loop over the working yarn and the top of the peg.

FIG8 st Take the working yarn behind the two pegs you will work the stitch over (we'll call them pegs 1 and 2). Wrap the yarn around to the front of peg 2, then thread it through pegs 1 and 2 to the center of the loom. Wrap the yarn around to the front of peg 1, then between pegs 1 and 2 to the center of the loom. Take bottom loop/stitch on peg 1 over the top stitch and top of the peg. For the next stitch, you will take the working yarn behind pegs 2 and 3 and repeat.

k Insert the knitting tool upward through the loop and grab the working yarn, keeping the working yarn to the outside of the frame. Pull the working yarn down through the loop, creating a new loop. Pull the loop off the peg and place the newly formed stitch on the peg.

k2tog Move loop from peg 1 to peg 2, move loops from outer pegs inward to fill the gap made by the move, keeping sts in their original order.

LTW Place loop from peg 1 on a stitch holder. Pick up the loop on peg 2 with your knitting tool and put it on peg 1. Now take the loop that is on the stitch holder and place it on peg 2. Knit both pegs.

M1 Move the last stitch in your row to the next empty peg. Reach below to the ladder stitch beneath the empty peg; lift this stitch and twist it. Place the newly formed stitch onto the empty peg. Work the next row as instructed in the pattern.

p Push the already existing loop to the top of the peg. Position the working yarn so it is beneath the loop on the peg. Insert the knitting pick down through the loop on the peg and grab the working yarn. Pull it through the loop on the peg to form a new loop. Pull the stitch off the peg and place the newly formed loop back on the peg.

PS   With the knitting tool, on the inside of the loom, reach down however many rows is indicated in the pattern and pick the stitch up directly in line with that peg. Place the stitch onto the peg, knit both stitches together as one, then pull gently down on your knitting to loosen the stitch a bit.

RTW   Place loop from peg 2 on a stitch holder. Pick up loop on peg 1 with your knitting tool and put it on peg 2. Now take the loop that is on the stitch holder and place it on peg 1. Knit both pegs.

ssk   Move peg 2 to peg 1, move loops from outer pegs inward to fill the gap made by the move, keeping sts in their original order.

u-k   Lay the working yarn above the existing loop on the peg and wrap it around the back of this same peg, creating a U. Pull the bottom loop over the working yarn and the top of the peg.

w&t   Knit or purl to where the w&t is called for; take the stitch off the next peg, and hold it with your knitting tool or fingers. Wrap the working yarn around the now-empty peg, wrapping from the back to the front of the peg. Place the stitch on your knitting tool back on the peg. With the working yarn, knit or purl back in the opposite direction without knitting the peg you did the w&t on. You will work those two stitches as one on the next row.

yo-k2tog/p2tog

Move peg 1 to peg 2, lay working yarn in front of peg 1, knit or purl the loops on peg 2 as one over working yarn.

Cable Stitches

4-st LC (4-stitch left cross)

1. Skip pegs 1 and 2. Knit your stitches on pegs 3 and 4.
2. Take stitches from pegs 3 and 4 and put them on a cable needle.
3. Knit loops on pegs 1 and 2.
4. Place loop from peg 1 on peg 3.
5. Place loop from peg 2 on peg 4.
6. Place loops from cable needle on pegs 1 and 2.
7. Tighten stitches on all pegs.

4-st RC (4-stitch right cross)

1. Place loops from pegs 1 and 2 on a cable needle.
2. Knit peg 3; then place it on peg 1.
3. Knit peg 4; then place it on peg 2.
4. Place loop 1 (on cable needle) and put it on peg 3; knit it.
5. Place loop 2 (on cable needle) and put it on peg 4; knit it.
6. Pull gently on all stitches to tighten.

6-st LC (6-stitch left cross)

1. Skip pegs 1, 2, and 3 by going behind them.
2. Knit loops on pegs 4, 5, and 6; keeping your stitches in order, place these stitches on a cable needle and hold in center of loom.
3. Knit pegs 1, 2, and 3.
4. Place loop from peg 3 on peg 6.
5. Place loop from peg 2 on peg 5.
6. Place loop from peg 1 on peg 4.
7. Place the loops on your cable needle on pegs 1, 2, and 3.
8. Gently pull loops on all pegs to tighten your stitches.

6-st RC (6-stitch right cross)

1. Place the loops from pegs 1, 2, and 3 on a cable needle.
2. Knit peg 4; place it on peg 1.
3. Knit peg 5; place it on peg 2.
4. Knit peg 6; place it on peg 3.
5. Take loop 1 (on cable needle), place it on peg 4; knit it.
6. Take loop 2 (on cable needle), place it on peg 5; knit it.
7. Take loop 3 (on cable needle), place it on peg 6; knit it.
8. Gently pull loops on all pegs to tighten your stitches.

QUICK ABBREVIATION GUIDE

*	Repeat instructions following *
4-st LC	4-stitch left cross
4-st RC	4-stitch right cross
6-st LC	6-stitch left cross
6-st RC	6-stitch right cross
BO	Bind off
CC	Coordinating or contrasting color
d-ewk	Double e-wrap knit
ew	E-wrap
ewk	E-wrap knit
ew-k2tog	E-wrap, knit 2 together
ew-p2tog	E-wrap, purl 2 together
ew-ssk	E-wrap, slip, slip knit
ew-ssp	E-wrap, slip, slip purl
FIG8 st	Figure 8 stitch
fl-k	Flat knit
k	Knit
k2tog	Knit 2 together

LTW	Left twist
M1	Make 1
MC	Main color
p	Purl
p2tog	Purl 2 together
PS	Puff stitch
rep	Repeat
RTW	Right twist
sk/sl	Skip/slip
ssk	Slip, slip knit
ssp	Slip, slip purl
st(s)	Stitch(es)
U-k	U-knit stitch
w&t	Wrap and turn
Yo	Yarn over
Yo-k2tog	Yarn over, knit 2 together
Yo-p2tog	Yarn over, purl 2 together